"Passionate, honest, and funny, Sarah Vermunt will take you from having no freaking idea what to do to being super jazzed and running down the path towards work that feels good. There *might* even be rainbows. There are so many YES! moments, so many nuggets of smarts and wisdom in this book. Each one is a little nudge; add them all up and you'll find yourself down the path of a fun and fulfilling career and, just maybe, actually liking Mondays."

Marc Johns, artist

"A fun, energizing, useful tool for the person who wants more from their work than a way to pay bills. Prepare to engage deeply and transform your work!"

Pamela Slim,
author of *Escape from Cubicle Nation* and *Body of Work*

"For those looking to throw their careers in the air and start fresh, *Careergasm* gives you a fun, friendly and . . . . approach of exactly how to do that. . . . . . . and laughing your way to . . . . th comedic and motivatio . . . . e there is more to life tha . . . . ou roll your eyes every Monday morr . . .

Jen Glantz, author of
Always a Bridesmaid (For Hire)

"With trademark wit and wisdom, Sarah Vermunt's *Career-gasm* calls out our passion and marries it to practicality to help us produce the kind of career we've all been dreaming of."

Christina Crook, author of
The Joy of Missing Out: Finding Balance in a Wired World

"A bible for anyone of any age who wants to take a career leap. My copy is lovingly filled with dog-eared pages so that I can come back to Sarah's wisdom over and over."

Tiffany Pratt,
designer and author of *This Can Be Beautiful*

CAREERGASM

Find Your Way

TO FEEL-GOOD
WORK

*Bullsh*t-Free
Advice to
Help You
Get After It*

SARAH VERMUNT

Published by ECW Press
665 Gerrard Street East
Toronto, Ontario, Canada, M4M 1Y2
416-694-3348 / info@ecwpress.com

Early versions of some of these chapters
were published at *Forbes, Inc.*, *Entrepreneur*,
and the *Huffington Post*.

LIBRARY AND ARCHIVES CANADA
CATALOGUING IN PUBLICATION

Vermunt, Sarah, 1980–, author
Careergasm : find your way to feel-good work /
Sarah Vermunt.

Issued in print and electronic formats.
ISBN 978-1-77041-371-9 (paperback)
ALSO ISSUED AS: 978-1-77090-988-5 (pdf)
978-1-77090-987-8 (epub)

1. Career changes. I. Title.

HF5384.V47 2017   650.14   C2016-
906345-3   C2016-906346-1

Editor for the press: Jen Knoch
Cover design: David A. Gee
Author photo: Anushila Shaw

The publication of *Careergasm* has been generously supported by the Government of Canada through the
Canada Book Fund. *Ce livre est financé en partie par le gouvernement du Canada.* We also acknowledge
the contribution of the Government of Ontario through the Ontario Book Publishing Tax Credit and the
Ontario Media Development Corporation.

ONTARIO ARTS COUNCIL
CONSEIL DES ARTS DE L'ONTARIO
an Ontario government agency
un organisme du gouvernement de l'Ontario

PRINTED AND BOUND IN CANADA

PRINTING: Marquis   5   4   3   2   1

MIX
Paper from
responsible sources
FSC
www.fsc.org   FSC® C103567

for
anyone
who
dreads
Monday
morning

What Is a Careergasm? ix

I QUIT *A Note from the Author* xi

1. LOOKING FOR CLUES 1

I Don't Know What I Want 2
And the Survey Says . . . 7
Activate Your Inner Toddler 12
Child Genius 17
Obsessed 21
Weird Is Good 26
Hey, Jealousy 30
Mason Jar Smoothie 35
Check Your Rearview Mirror 39

2. YOUR SECRET INGREDIENTS 43

Iron Chef 44
I Can't Work in
     These Conditions! 48
Hot and Cold 53
More Happy or Less Happy? 57
You Do You 62
Embrace Your Inner Molly
     Ringwald 67

3. THE RESISTANCE 73

Just Gimme a Sign 74
You Can't Quarantine Desire 79
Welcome to the Resistance 83
Excuses, Excuses 88
I'm Fine, Really 93

4. BURNOUT, BAGGAGE, & BREAKDOWNS 97

Snap 98
The Burnout Club 102
Gut Check 108
Surrender 113
Check Your Baggage 117
Selfish 123

5. FEAR 129

Careerhack 130
Fear Disguised as Practicality 134
Is All Fear Bad? 138
Fearless, My Ass 140

6. AMBITION 145

Don't Fight Your Curves 146
$UCCE$$ 150
Easy There, Tiger 153
Enough Is Enough 157
Enlightened Ambition 161
The Seduction of Should 168
Ambition Amnesia 171
Even Better 178

7. MONEY 183

The Cheesemaker
    and the iPhone 184
A Van Down by the River 189
The Shitty End of the Stick 193
Who's the Boss? 196

8. FAILURE 203

Worst-Case Scenario 204
The Agony of Defeat 209
Plan B 213
Don't Apologize 218

9. EVERYBODY'S TWO CENTS 223

What Will People Think? 224
Where Is the Parade
    I Ordered? 229
Angels and Assholes 233
Watch Your Language 237

10. BEGINNING 241

Make Room 242
Amateur 246
Glamorous, It's Not 251
Get in the Game 255
Al dente 260

YOU'RE INVITED *A Send-Off* 267

Acknowledgments 270
About the Author 272

WHAT IS A
CAREERGASM?

What is a Careergasm? Does it feel as good as it sounds?

You bet your ass it does. A careergasm happens when your work feels good. Like, *really* good. Like a groovin' Marvin Gaye song. Like you and your work *belong* together. It happens when you feel connected to your work — when you choose it, and it chooses you — and when you want to keep coming back for more.

When you're on the right career path, it feels like a vocation, a calling. You feel like you're doing exactly what you're meant to do and what comes naturally to you. Your work leaves you feeling happy and satisfied and full — not every day, but most of the time.

A careergasm happens when you want the one you're with. You've got a hot date every Monday morning, and you show up over and over and over again because it just feels right.

It's hard to describe a careergasm to someone who has never had one. All you can do is smile knowingly and say, "Just you wait. It's amazing. And worth every bit of effort it takes to get there." Because it *does* take effort. Like anything good, you have to work at it. This book will help you do the work you need to do to get there.

Maybe you've had a careergasm before, but things have fizzled out. You've lost that lovin' feelin'. If your work used to be hot, and now it's not, it's either time to spice things up or time to move on. Some things aren't meant to stay in our lives forever. That includes old passions that have burned out. Maybe it's time to let go and move in another direction.

But how do you get your mojo back when you're in a passionless relationship with your work? One step at a time, baby. Every day there are people all over the world doing just that — letting go and taking a bold step in a new direction. I'm here to help you take yours. It's time to feel good again.

I QUIT
A NOTE FROM THE AUTHOR

I had a breakdown in the middle of a crowded Starbucks.

I was working on my dissertation. I hated it. I had hated it for a long time, but on that day something in me just broke. I was miserable, and my capacity for faking interest — even *mild* interest — in something I hated was exhausted. I couldn't do it anymore. Not for another second. I don't know why it happened at that particular time on that particular day. I didn't see it coming. Maybe I should have, but I didn't.

I felt myself start to unravel. My stomach twisted, and I felt an icy hot flash of panic pulse through my body. To my horror, I made a scene. I cried. We're not talking a quiet, single-tear cry. We're talking the fast and furious flood kind, with a snotty nose and choppy, heaving breaths. I was shaking so hard I nearly spilled my coffee all over my laptop. I rushed to gather my things so I could leave and save myself the public embarrassment, but it was too late. I watched the whole affair unfold from up above, outside of my own body. I thought, *So this is what a breakdown looks like*. It was awful. And exactly what I needed.

The next day I walked into my Ph.D. supervisor's office and told him I was quitting, four years into my Ph.D. and 93 pages into my dissertation. I'd keep my teaching job until the end of the year, but I was leaving. A career as a professor was not for me.

I was afraid of what people would think. I was afraid I'd look like a failure. I was afraid I'd lose everything I'd worked for. I was afraid it would kill me.

But I did it anyway. I listened to the little voice.

I am so proud of that decision. It's the hardest decision I've ever made, and one of the best. Quitting was a gift I finally found the guts to give myself.

That happened four years ago, and since then I've devoted my life to helping people quit jobs they hate, to helping them get the hell out of Dodge when they just can't take it anymore. I took all of that experience from teaching at a business school and spun it into something new, something that feels *way* better. That broken-down woman at Starbucks is now a career coach, helping other people to take their power back and choose something better.

If you're lost or struggling or unhappy in your work, know that I know what that feels like. So do a lot of people. *Gallup*, *Forbes*, and the *New York Times* report that more than half of Americans are unhappy and disengaged in their work. What most of us don't realize is that your breaking point is actually freedom calling.

In the following pages, it's my hope to help you find the strength to turn away from work you hate and the courage to move toward work you love. I'm going to help you ask the right questions, dig deep, and figure out what you actually want. I'm also going to help you address your fear and resistance so you can say, *Fuck it. Yes, I'm terrified, but it's worth it. Let's do this.*

xo
Sarah

P.S. I changed the names and identifying details of pretty much everyone in this book. Because I'm not an asshole. May their stories, and my own, give you the loving kick in the pants you need to find your way to feel-good work.

LOOKING
FOR CLUES

YOU'LL NEVER FIND WHAT YOU'RE LOOKING FOR
IF YOU KEEP LOOKING IN THE WRONG PLACE.

I DON'T
KNOW WHAT I WANT

People say one of the hardest things to do in the pursuit of a happy career is figure out what kind of work you actually want to do. I agree with that.

Kind of.

In fact, I'd say it's something more like this: One of the hardest things to do in the pursuit of a happy career is *admitting to yourself* what kind of work you actually want to do. There's a big difference between not knowing what you want and not admitting what you want.

Most of the people who come to me for career coaching feel lost. They don't know what they want. At least, they *think* they don't know what they want. But more than half of the time — hell, *most* of the time — the problem has nothing to do with knowing; it's the fear associated with desire.

There's nothing more terrifying than admitting what you actually want — especially if you think you can't have it.

For most, the problem isn't that you don't know what you want. It's that you're scared shitless to want it. Admitting that you want something means doing something about it. It means you're either going to be on the hook for making it happen, or going to knowingly let yourself down. And I don't even have to tell you which of those two outcomes is tougher on you in the long run.

> There's nothing more terrifying than admitting what you actually want — especially if you think you can't have it.

Saying you don't know what you want is easier because it makes you the poor schmuck who's in the dark. *But I would toooootally pursue my passion if only I knew what it was.* Is that really true? I'd be willing to bet that on some level, there is a very wise part of you that knows exactly what you want.

Some people live their whole lives trying to hide from their own truth. Don't go through life willingly playing the part of the poor schmuck.

Here's what I'm talking about:

BANKER: I've got to get out of this god-forsaken profession, but I don't know what I want to do.
ME: What kind of work do you think would make you happy?
BANKER: I don't know.
ME: [*activating stern librarian glare*] Is that really true? You have no idea what would make you happy?
BANKER: Yes. I don't know.
ME: [*radio silence + raised eyebrow* (the facial equivalent of calling double bullshit)]
BANKER: Okay. I've actually always wanted to be a brewmaster, but I can't do *that*!

BINGO.

If this resonates with you, then, honey, your problem is not that you don't know what you want. It's that you're afraid to want it. And those are two very different things.

Think the banker-turned-brewmaster example is far-fetched? Think again. A client of mine made that exact transition. And he did it several years into his profession, and while raising two young boys. He even took a crappy minimum wage job at a brewery one summer, so he could learn the industry. He was paying the nanny more per hour to watch the kids than he was making. If you're afraid to let yourself want what you want because you think you can't have it, just remember the banker-turned-brewmaster.

Consider the following question, and answer it honestly:

Are you really as lost as you think you are,
or are you just afraid?

Maybe that question feels like a relief to you. Maybe you're thinking, *OMG, deep down I DO know what I want, but I don't know how to get it. I'm terrified!*

Or maybe that question really pisses you off. Maybe you're thinking, *Listen, lady, you have no idea how much I've struggled with this. I really DON'T know what I want, and I'm trying really fucking hard to figure it out.* If this is you, hang in there. I'm going to help you return to the part of yourself that knows.

If you truly don't know what you want, chances are you lost touch with your desire somewhere along the way. At some point in time, you pushed that desire waaaaay down to a place where you're now able to tell yourself, convincingly, that you don't know what you want. Maybe you did this after college, or when you started a family. Maybe earlier. Maybe you pushed that desire down when you were an anxious teenager worried about your future, or when you were an obedient child trying your best to show your parents love and gratitude, no matter the cost. You may have pushed that desire down so long ago that you don't even know how to access it anymore.

But it's there. And if you're willing, I can help you find it.

AND
THE SURVEY SAYS . . .

Have you ever taken one of those aptitude inventories that tells you what you should be when you grow up? You know the kind. *Based on this 10-minute survey, you're destined to be either an accountant or a lion tamer!*

These types of assessments can be comforting and are sometimes a good starting point, but without some more introspection they're also often the reason why people get stuck in the wrong career. When it comes time to make a career decision, many people take the easy road and do what an assessment tells them to do, with little further inquiry.

Maybe you took that road, too. Maybe you picked your career based on what you were told to do by a career inventory, or an aptitude test, or a personality assessment . . .

or a guidance counselor, friend, parent, spouse, teacher, or mentor. These people all probably had the best of intentions, but they had no real way of knowing what's best for *you*. Only you know that.

On the one hand, that's awesome! As Glinda the Good Witch would say, "You had the power all along!" On the other hand, *Holy pressure*, *Batman*. That's why so many people cave to someone else's career advice: It *seems* easier. But sometimes the easy road actually gets you lost, even when you follow directions and do everything "right."

Have you ever done that? Followed someone else's directions only to get lost? It's infuriating. You probably could have done your own navigation and been just fine, but it seemed safer, more prudent, to get directions from someone else, just to make sure you're going the right way. Then when you get lost, you think, *WTF?! I thought these directions were supposed to get me where I wanted to go!*

Sometimes you take direction from others and get exactly where you were supposed to go — only when you get there, it looks nothing like you thought it would. You think, *This is it? THIS is the place I've been working so hard to get to? What a letdown.* You want to get the hell out of there, but you have no idea which way to turn. You've "arrived," but you're also lost.

If you're feeling lost in your career, chances are you'll have to dig a little deeper to see which path is best for you.

Sometimes the easy road actually gets you lost, even when you follow directions and do everything "right."

When a highway is about to be resurfaced, first the road has to be milled — you have to dig beneath the surface and expose what's underneath to make a foundation so the new road will actually stick. The milled road is kind of bumpy and corrugated, like corduroy. The old road has to be ground away before the new one can be laid.

It's the same for buildings. You have to dig beneath the surface to build a foundation. This is the most important step. If you get the foundation wrong, you can't properly support what you build.

What do roads and buildings have to do with your career? On the off chance that you're in construction, lots. On the more likely chance that you're not, this: *If you want to build something that will last, you're going to have to dig deep first.*

You need to get in touch with what you actually want. What you want will be different from what I want, and what your mother wants, and what your best friend wants. That's why following someone else's advice (whether it's dispensed by your dad or a guidance counselor or a

> If you want to build something
> that will last, you're going
> to have to dig deep first.

sophisticated career assessment) doesn't always work. You are unique: Nobody but *you* can get it right.

We're not meant to be pigeonholed: You're one of a kind, and your career should be, too.

ACTIVATE
YOUR INNER TODDLER

If you have a toddler, or know one, or were one once, you know that they are *not* shy about expressing their feelings. They can go from squeals of delight to a raging hissy fit in 10 seconds flat . . . and vice versa.

A new Spiderman action figure? Pure joy! But ask him to share it with his little sister, and you've got a miniature Godzilla on your hands.

Toddlers aren't very concerned with social norms. They wear their feelings on the outside. They're still relatively new to the planet, so they haven't picked up all of the rules yet. And is that really such a bad thing?

As adults, we play by the rules and do what's expected of us. We're polite, proper, and professional. We don't do a happy dance in the middle of a crowded street. We don't cry and kick and scream in a vocal range audible only to dogs.

Well, aren't you a little bit sick of that? Aren't there times when you want to kick and scream and make a scene because you have to do something you hate? And aren't there times when you want to squeal with delight and do a goofy little jig, but you don't because you're afraid people will think you've flipped your lid?

When it comes to your career — and, hell, when it comes to life — I think we'd be better off if we embraced our inner toddlers a little more often.

Now, I'm not suggesting that you call your boss a poo-poo head (if you must, please line up another job first), or pout and stomp around when you don't get that promotion (okay, maybe in private). I'm simply suggesting that you *notice* what makes you want to throw a raging fit. *Notice* what makes you want to squeal with delight. These are MAJOR clues on the path to feel-good work.

A friend of mine is a business consultant with a big firm. They have lots of rules — even rules about her shoes. She's allowed to wear pointy-toed high heels, but not square-toed ones. When I hear this, I think, *OMG, kill me now*. I would never survive there. That is just too many rules for me — not to mention ridiculous.

Stupid rules make me want to throw a hissy fit. Other things on my hissy fit list include pointless meetings, mindless small talk, annoying jargon, networking events, and boring research journals. All of these things make me want to throw myself on the ground and carry on like a toddler who's just been told it's time to leave the splash pad.

What's on your hissy fit list? Think about it. What rules do you long to stop following? What do you wish you never had to do again? What makes you want to flop around like a fish in the candy aisle of a crowded grocery store?

Go ahead and make a list. Include things from your work life that you hate, but feel free to add other things, too. Non work-related things on my hissy fit list: wine (I've tried to like it for years, but I think it's gross and I'm sick of trying to like it just because everyone else does) and messy spaces (the thought of curling up and watching Netflix in a room with yesterday's dirty dishes within sight gives me hives).

Now, let's look at the other side of the inner toddler spectrum: squeals of delight. What lights you up? What makes you feel like a kid with a bag of Skittles and a Kool-Aid-stained grin?

I'm talking about work things *and* non-work things. Some things on my squeals of delight list: bright nail polish, rivers and mountains, alone time, pretty stationery, writing, deep conversation, beautiful design, organizing, planning, nurturing others, problem solving, and working with delightful people one-on-one.

If you look at both of your lists, you'll probably notice some themes. Don't expect a specific job title to pop out at you. We're not there yet. Just look at your lists and see if any themes emerge.

Need some help? I'll show you what I mean. Let's take a look at my own lists.

My hissy fit list tells me that I'm *reeeeeally* not into shallow connections or interactions. It also tells me that I'm not into traditional corporate stuff, and that doing something just because it's conventional makes me feel like crap.

My squeals of delight list suggests that I like things that are fun and a little bit kooky. I'm also a visual person. Art and design matter to me. And space and nature make me feel good.

What makes you feel like a kid with a bag of Skittles and a Kool-Aid-stained grin?

Return to your own lists and see what you can learn. It should be obvious, but I'll go ahead and say it anyway: Put some distance between yourself and the stuff on your hissy fit list, and move toward the things that feel like pure delight.

But I can't stop doing the things I hate!
That would mean a total overhaul!

Uh . . . yeah. Maybe that's exactly what you need.

And I can't devote more time to stuff I love.
It's not practical! People will think I'm nuts!

Dude. Who cares? This is your life we're talking about. You're supposed to enjoy it. It's time you took your life back. Embrace your inner toddler. Live a little. I'll meet you by the splash pad.

CHILD
GENIUS

You may feel like you've lost your connection with the things you used to be passionate about. You might even forget what they were. But you can reconnect with some of your natural passions if you look back far enough into your past. Like, *waaaaay* back, to when you were eight years old. There's career navigation gold back there.

What did you love to do when you were eight?

Seriously, think about it.

When I was eight, I loved to play teacher. I loved to organize lessons and I loved to give away stickers. Okay, maybe it was mostly about the stickers. I had a pretty awesome sticker collection. My favorite one smelled like grape.

I loved taking care of animals, too. Kittens, in particular. There's a photo of me as a kid on my tricycle with a sandcastle bucket dangling from the handlebars and a kitten tucked into the bucket. That poor kitten was probably terrified, but my heart was in the right place.

I also *loooooved* to make stuff. Any stuff. Crafts were my thing. I made things with pipe cleaners and beads and brought them to craft shows with my mom. Bless the kind little old ladies who paid me a quarter for them. It made my heart soar.

What games and activities did you love as a kid? These things will have no obvious connection with your career, and that's okay. My pipe-cleaner-and-bead doohickey hobby was not exactly scalable, and as of yet I have been unable to build a viable business giving tricycle rides to kittens (still crossing my fingers, though).

Forget about the career implications for now, and just think about the stuff you used to love as a kid. Can't remember? Ask a parent or sibling. Other things on my own list include coloring, reading, writing stories and plays, sewing my own scrunchies, making collages, and looking for critters in the creek (pronounced "crick," if you want to say it the proper country girl way). Some of my clients say their favorite things were Legos, puzzles, building sandcastles, baseball, soccer, playing dress-up, making forts, painting, playing cops and robbers.

When you think about the stuff you loved as a kid, do you see any themes emerge? What are your childhood passions trying to tell you? For example, is a lot of that stuff creative? Outdoorsy? Analytical? Nurturing? Solitary? Social?

Does it involve building? Problem solving? Logic? Using your hands? Helping people? Making something? Adventure? Imagination? You see where I'm going with this.

Themes like these are clues for finding a feel-good career. If you loved it when you were eight, chances are there's something you love about it *still*.

If you loved it when you were eight, chances are there's something you love about it *still*.

Also try to remember what things you were most proud of. My standout moments include a second-grade story about the Easter Bunny and a pair of Air Jordan shoes, and writing and performing in a bunch of student council skits, in which I usually cast myself as either Dr. Evil from *Austin Powers* or Brain from *Pinky and the Brain*.

Were you a star athlete? An artist? A musician? An actor? An entertainer? A builder? A leader? An advocate? A nurturer? A change-maker? A creative thinker? A communicator? A public speaker? A debater? A researcher? A writer? A scientist? A designer? An organizer? A relation-ship builder? A director? A documentarian? An academic?

What exactly were you proud of, and why? Think of a few examples.

Now, I took pride in my Easter Bunny Air Jordan story and my wacky plays based on '90s characters, not because I was destined to do that forever, but because there's a connection to creativity and writing there. As it turns out, those things are really important for me in my career.

If there's a unifying theme that emerges and links some of the things you were proud of as a kid or a teenager, it *means* something — even now, all these years later.

It's possible that somewhere along the way, you convinced yourself (or more likely someone else did) that the things that make you proud and bring you fulfillment are silly. Or impractical. Or not of value.

Bullshit.

You need to invite fulfillment back into your life. It isn't silly. It's not impractical. It *does* have value. You need to find a way back to the things that fill you up — because wouldn't it be awesome if your career felt like one big playdate?

OBSESSED

My brother Brad has an undergraduate degree in mathematics and a master's degree in biology. Right now you're probably picturing him working as a scientist and wearing a white lab coat at work every day. If so, you're wrong. Dead wrong.

He's a television writer.

For as long as I can remember, Brad has been obsessed with television. Not the "get home from work and slump in front of the tube for hours of mindless consumption" kind of thing (that's just numbing out). Brad was always, and continues to be, an engaged television enthusiast, especially television comedy.

He could (and does) watch, analyze, discuss, critique, and create television for several hours every day. He gets caught up in it and loses all track of time when he's fully immersed in it. I can't think of anything he loves to do more.

Brad probably could have had a steady gig with great pay working in the sciences after completing his master's degree. He's a smart guy with a talent for math and science, and he's even had some of his research published in scientific journals. But that's not what he wanted for his career.

He didn't exactly hate biology, but he didn't love it either. In his spare time during his degree, he wrote spec scripts as a hobby. He wrote, filmed, acted in, and edited a web series and a cable-access sketch comedy series. None of this made him any money. He just loved it so much that he felt compelled to do it.

Impractical and far-fetched as it seemed, Brad decided to change course completely to try to make his television writer dream a reality. He graduated with his master's degree in biology on a Friday and began his studies in film and television writing the next Monday. He poured what little money he had into it. He lived in a shitty apartment and worked part-time as a math tutor to make it happen. It wasn't (and still isn't) glamorous or lucrative, but now he's doing what he loves and getting paid for it.

A former colleague of mine, Krissy, has long been fascinated by and obsessed with wine. And I'm not talking about popping a bottle every night to dull the ache of a stressful day — she is a bona fide wine *nut*. She loves everything about wine — the way the wine world is always evolving, so there's always something to learn; and how there are never really wrong answers because taste is so subjective; and how wine can transport you to another time and place, just like an old song.

Krissy used to work as a recruiter. Now she works in the wine industry. She picked up her entire life and made the 2,500-mile move from Toronto to Summerland, British Columbia, to pursue a career in wine. She reinvented her career entirely (a gutsy move!), and the life she has built with her partner and her beautiful daughter is nothing short of inspiring. I smile every time I see her happy updates pop up on Facebook and Instagram.

I know a woman who is a natural born artist. She's *always* been an artist at heart, but while her parents appreciated art, they told her that "the artist thing is for other people, not you." This message stayed with her for 30 years into her career as she pursued various "practical" options, most recently in academia. For her Ph.D. dissertation defense, she wanted to visually transform her research into dissolving points of light, like a disco ball (which is certainly not the norm). She is whip-smart and incredibly knowledgeable, but a traditional dissertation felt too constraining to her. It *had* to be communicated through art. It was the only way. I asked her, "Is it possible you're an artist and not an academic?" She is now pursuing more of her art and leaning further into the arts in her career. Finally! It only took her 30 years!

Another woman, Anushila, fell in love with photography during college, but she was convinced to study law because she believed it was a safer track — jobs were for money and passions could be hobbies. So she went to law school, kicked ass, and got an enviable gig at a big law firm in New York. But she soon realized she didn't like the life of a law firm associate. One of the things Anushila did to cope with feeling stuck in the wrong profession was to play with photography again. She didn't have much time for it, but it felt like an escape, and it brought her joy. Even while working in law, she began to pursue photography seriously. Some of her work was short-listed for *National Geographic*. *National Geographic*! The photographer's gold standard! She eventually decided to leave law and pursue photography full-time. She has her own business now, is a published fashion photographer, and is doing her master's in fashion photography in New York. I couldn't be happier for her.

Is there something in your life that you're obsessed with? Some kind of persistent fascination or curiosity?

Lean in to your
obsessions and fascinations.
Indulge your passions.

What makes you lose track of time? When have you been so completely engaged in an activity that you felt fully energized, like you could go on forever?

Those things are clues. Lean in to your obsessions and fascinations. Indulge your passions. Who knows where they might lead you?

WEIRD
IS GOOD

Like the song says, people are strange.

Sure, we look pretty normal-ish when we're dressed in suits and jackets on the way to work, but when we get home and let loose with the people we love, we're a bit kooky.

We're kung fu masters, party planners, gadget builders, poets, puppeteers, Tough Mudder champions, urban farmers, and yarn bombers.

There are a lot of wackadoodle talents out there, and that's a good thing! Those weird and wacky talents of yours offer some clues about your best career path.

What are your talents and gifts, however strange?

I mean anything that you're good at that you love to do. And I mean *anything*. Career-related or not. Juggling.

Arranging flowers. Sewing costumes. Making photo collages of your cat. Hula hooping. Doodling. Making the perfect green smoothie. You'll probably come up with things that have no fathomable connection to making you money. That's good. We're going to get creative here.

To get your gears turning, here are a couple of my own weird gifts that are (seemingly) unrelated to my work:

I'm crafty. Not the sly and underhanded kind of crafty — the ink stamp and glitter glue kind. I can whip up a handmade Christmas card like nobody's business. Don't even get me started on collages and fancy gift-wrapping.

I can recommend exactly the right book to the right person at the right time. Almost once a week, someone says something like, *Holy shit, Sarah! That book is EXACTLY what I needed. How did you know?*

I'm suuuuuper organized. Like, borderline OCD organized. From my computer desktop to my home, there's a place and a system for everything.

Do these weird gifts mean that I should start a stationery line, or a book recommendation service, or a closet design company? Well, I certainly *could* do those things. But if we dig deeper, we can see what's *behind* these weird gifts.

My crafty nature is really rooted in the fact that I'm a visual person. I don't have the chops (or patience) to be a designer, but I can assemble and arrange visual objects in really interesting and creative ways. I use this weird gift in my career when I use design to support my business, whether it's pulling together my website, composing blog photos, or using social media. It's all very visual and reflects my own personal aesthetic.

My ability to consistently recommend good books for others is really rooted in my ability to listen and relate to people. I'm able to listen to their concerns, notice what they seem to be yearning for, and recall a piece of information from a book they might relate to. As it turns out, listening is one of the most important skills I use when coaching my clients.

What about my freakish compulsion to organize everything? Well, I happen to get geek-out giddy when using systems. I see the world in ordered systems. I put this to use when I design a course or help an aspiring entrepreneur develop her business plan.

Maybe you get a high from spreadsheets and numbers and making sense of complex data.

Maybe you're calm amid chaos and seem to be at your best when the work around you is turbulent.

Maybe you're a plant whisperer, and people are always shocked and amazed when you can bring anything green back to life.

Maybe people — even people you just met — are always coming to you for advice and guidance because of the nurturing energy you radiate.

Whatever your weird gifts are, embrace them. Then ask yourself, *What's behind this weird gift?* What talent or skill does this weird gift stem from? And how might it provide value for someone else? Get creative. Chances are you can weave some of those wacky talents into a feel-good career.

When we don't use our gifts, there's a heaviness we carry in our hearts and minds.

A feel-good career is one that honors the best of what you have to offer. That's why it's important to embrace your strange talents and weird gifts. Leaving them out of your career is a missed opportunity on so many levels — a missed opportunity to serve others, a missed opportunity for creativity and innovation, and certainly a missed opportunity to invite more happiness into your life.

One of my favorite authors, Elizabeth Gilbert, says that a monk once told her, "Any talent that we have but do not use becomes a burden." I agree with that. When we don't use our gifts, there's a heaviness we carry in our hearts and minds. When we *do* use them, there's a lightness about our work. There's ease, synchronicity and satisfaction. That's what I want for you.

HEY,
JEALOUSY

Be honest. You get jealous sometimes.

Me too.

It's not the most glamorous or commendable emotion, but let's just go ahead and admit that we all feel jealous sometimes. Okay? Okay.

Maybe you're jealous of your brother who just made a radical career change. Meanwhile, you hate your job.

Maybe you're jealous of your coworker's kickass all-star presentation. Especially when you feel like nobody even notices your work.

Maybe you're jealous of your friend who finally found the guts to quit her job and start her own business. Ballsy.

There are probably some people you love/hate because they're doing super cool shit — and why the hell can't you do that, too? Amiright?

I'll admit that I'm a wee bit jealous of some big, badass coaches who are doing big, badass things that I wish I was doing — international tours and million-dollar product launches. I'm jealous of anyone who can give a keynote speech without wanting to puke backstage beforehand. I'm jealous of people who don't seem to give a flying fuck about what other people think, and just do their own damn thing, anxiety-free.

A friend of mine, Jessie, is jealous of her former colleague's new career working in an art gallery. She thinks, *I wish I was doing that!* while she continues to slog away at her crappy administrative job.

James is jealous of his ex-girlfriend who downsized her life and now lives on a houseboat. He thinks, *Must be nice, but I could never do that* . . . as he continues to buy more stuff he doesn't need and will probably never use.

Tasha is jealous of Mo, who just wrote and produced his own play. She thinks, *Why can't I get my shit together and do that, too?!* She's thought about writing her own play about a hundred times.

As far as emotions go, jealousy sucks. There's an uncomfortable dissonance in yearning deeply for something but not allowing yourself to go after it. It's a pretty crappy feeling.

But what if you could turn your jealousy into a tool? What if you could use this painful emotion to your benefit and make it a teacher? There's a part of jealousy that makes this possible. *Not* — ahem — the part that makes you want to stab someone in the neck, or "accidentally" spill your hot coffee on them (that's the unhealthy part). I'm talking about the *desire* part.

Access the yearning, burning desire part of your jealousy. Embrace your green-eyed monster. It's trying to tell you something.

Think of the people whose career you're jealous of. Make a list if you want. Go ahead, nobody's watching.

Now, what is your jealousy trying to tell you? What is it exactly that you want? There's probably a particular thing about each person who came to mind that really gets your jealousy jacked up.

Maybe someone you're jealous of seems like they're having way too much fun to be earning so much money (perhaps that tells you that you want to have more fun at work). Maybe another person you're jealous of is really good at something you struggle with (perhaps that tells you that you want to master that particular skill). See where I'm going with this?

Jealousy isn't really about the other person. It's always about you.

You don't have to let your jealousy get the best of you.

Let it teach you something about your own desire, and suddenly it becomes a tool. It can help you notice what you want. Once you're clear on that, it's up to you to find the guts to go out there and get it.

This whole idea works for people you're a superfan of, too. You know those people — the people you worship and follow. Maybe they're celebrities, maybe they're people you know and love, but for whatever reason, you are sooooo drinking their Kool-Aid.

Jealousy isn't really about the other person. It's always about you.

I'm a mega fangirl of Oprah. But what is it about her that I love? The thought of being on TV scares the living shit out of me, so it's certainly not the media empire thing. I think it's the fact that she's nurturing and real, and she helps other people live their best lives. I look at her and I think, *Yes! I gotta get me somma that!*

I'm also insanely inspired by anything written by author Danielle LaPorte. She cuts right down to the truth. No bullshit. Plus, the woman writes like a rock star.

I love quirky art created by Marc Johns. A lot of his art manages to strike a balance between whimsy and wise. I totally dig that unexpected combo.

Who are you a superfan of? Think about it for a second.

You may not have considered it, but your superfan status can teach you a thing or two about your career desires. What is it about the people you adore and idolize that makes you dig their mojo? And what does that tell you about your own desire?

Rock that inner superfan, my friend. You'll find yourself getting a little closer to being someone your current self is jealous of.

MASON
JAR SMOOTHIE

Every once in a while, on a day when I'm not running late for work and rushing to feed the cat before I scoot out the door, I'll make myself a green smoothie to start my day. I'll pour that sucker into a mason jar, and I'll think, *Dammit, that right there is a thing of beauty*. Then I'll take a photo of it and share it on Instagram.

I don't drink green smoothies every day. And I have no legitimate reason for owning mason jars. I just think they look cool. I don't make things like pickled beets, or home-made relish, or even jam. I eat things like cereal, and Zoodles, and leftover Chinese food for dinner on a regular basis.

But I'm not Instagraming my Zoodles. I'm not taking a selfie as I scarf a sandwich while hunched over my

35

computer, but I will if I'm making homemade chicken soup, or toasted coconut pancakes, or a gorgeous green smoothie in a mason jar.

Why do I do this? For the same reason everyone else does. We want to share the cool stuff. Zoodles and leftover Chinese don't quite make the cut. A selfie while you're kicking ass at the gym seems share-worthy. So does a pic of you with your newborn niece, or the *Mona Lisa*, or your dog dressed as a taco for Halloween. But a selfie alone with your cats as you fold laundry on a Saturday night? Not so much. (Now, if your cats are *helping* you fold your laundry, that's another story.)

You may read about someone's love for event management on their LinkedIn profile, but you don't see them cursing under their breath when they're still setting up the trade show booth onsite at 2:30 a.m., delirious from exhaustion six-and-a-half hours before the venue opens to the public. And that Facebook photo of your entrepreneur friend at a café in Paris on a Wednesday afternoon? She probably didn't mention that she only spent 15 minutes at the café and the rest of her 14-hour day in taxis, conference rooms, and airports.

My point? We are all occasionally full of shit. That's okay. It's human to want to share the cool stuff and not the mundane. Plus, nobody really wants to see you opening your mail, or sorting socks, or cleaning out your purse. That shit is boring. That's why we don't share it. But let's keep it real — life is not a café au lait in Paris or a mason jar smoothie. Our public lives — especially what we share on social media — are finely curated highlight reels. Of course you know this. We all know this. But sometimes we also forget it. And it's so important to keep in mind as you're lusting after someone else's glamorous career from a distance. We only see the best version of what everybody else is up to.

We are all occasionally full of shit.

I came across an article in *Adweek* about a couple who quit their advertising jobs to follow their dreams and travel the world, picking up work along the way to fund The Dream. They posted photos of cliff jumping, beach yoga, waterfalls, cobblestone streets, vintage cars, and Greek columns. They were an Instagram sensation. One of their sailing photos included the caption, "Sailing is so much more than a luxurious pastime or hobby — it's a lifestyle."

Sounds pretty great, right? Sign me up! But six months into their travels, they wrote a blog post admitting the brutal reality behind the shiny photos: they were funding their travels by scrubbing toilets, shoveling rocks, making beds, spreading manure, and scooping dog poop. Their situation was a lot shittier (quite literally) than their Instagram feed would have you believe. They were barely making enough money to buy food, and the jobs they were taking were anything but glamorous.

It's fun to see what other people are up to in their work and their lives. Social media lets us do that. I love watching from a digital distance, but I take all of it with a rather large grain of salt. You should, too. In fact, some people's public personas require an entire salt mine. If you're researching potential careers or following the careers and lifestyles of others, make sure you're working with real information.

Supplement the storybook versions of the careers and lifestyles you see on social media with real, firsthand information. Talk to people who are doing the work you want to do. Talk to many of them, and talk to them in real life, face-to-face if you can. The more you do this, the more likely you are to get some real information. You'll be able to tell the difference between the people who are blowing smoke up your ass and the people who are giving you the real, unfiltered truth. The grass (or, indeed, the smoothie) always seems greener on Instagram, but it rarely is.

CHECK
YOUR REARVIEW MIRROR

You can't see what's in front of you by looking in the rearview mirror.

True. But you *do* have to check the rearview mirror while driving. Looking behind you gives you helpful information as you navigate the road ahead.

Of course, I'm not just talking about driving. Looking behind you can be damn helpful for your career, too.

Consider your career up until now. You can mine your work history — all of it, even the shitty jobs — for precious clues about what your ideal career could look like.

If you hate your job or industry, you might feel like your career up until now has been wasted time. Trust me — while it may feel that way, there are good clues there.

When you use your work history as a teaching tool, the dots start to connect. You notice that your previous experiences were there to teach you something about yourself, and making a career change, even a radical one, no longer feels like you've been wasting years of your life. It's *all* valuable stuff.

Think about all of the jobs you've ever had. Even the volunteer jobs, part-time gigs, extracurriculars, student jobs, babysitting, burger flipping, whatever. Go as far back as you can remember — even back to the jobs you had as a teenager and young adult. Write 'em down if you need to.

You can mine your work history — all of it, even the shitty jobs — for precious clues about what your ideal career could look like.

Now, think of one or two things you genuinely liked about each of your former jobs. This is hard for jobs you hated, but there was probably *something* you enjoyed about each gig. For example, when I was a teenager, I worked at a meat counter. I hated that job, but I did enjoy cleaning the shop and keeping things organized. It was a very small part of the job, but for me it was the best part. I wasn't especially psyched about my babysitting job either (I was actually a pretty terrible babysitter), but I *did* love raiding the cupboard for snacks and watching soap operas when the kids were down for a nap.

The best job I ever had, aside from the one I have now, was way back during my undergrad degree, when I worked as a residence assistant in a university dorm. People came to me with their problems. I created a community of support. The pay was crappy, and the hours were many, but I could write a list a mile long of the things I loved about that job.

I've had jobs working as a waitress, a cleaner, a shop-keeper, a salesperson, a reporter, a recruiter, a manager, a trainer, a marketer, an advisor, a receptionist, an editor, a speaker, a researcher, a professor, a writer, and a coach. Based only on what I *liked* about these jobs (not the job titles or job descriptions), some of the themes I notice are creating, organizing, nurturing, helping, teaching, and communicating. These are my own personal career history signposts — things I love that keep showing up over and over again.

Think back to the stuff you liked about your previous jobs. What themes emerge? Those themes are *your* career history signposts — what you might consider important ingredients for a fulfilling career. Try to work in as much of that stuff as you can.

Don't see many of those ingredients in your current career? Maybe it's time for a bigger change.

YOUR SECRET INGREDIENTS

FORGET ABOUT WORKING FROM SOMEONE
ELSE'S RECIPE. MAKE YOUR OWN.

IRON
CHEF

Do you remember the show *Iron Chef*? A bunch of world-class chefs would do a cook-off using specific theme ingredients. Even with the same ingredients, each chef would whip up something totally different from what the guy beside him created. I love cooking shows where the chefs don't work from exact recipes. They take a handful of this, a bunch of that, a dab of something else, and voilà: a delicious meal.

You can do that with your career, too.

So let's forget about job titles for a minute. Let's talk about career *ingredients* instead — because the truth is, you don't need to know exactly what your ideal job looks like in order to identify some of the main ingredients that would make a really satisfying career.

One of my clients, Jason, wants to stay within the same industry, but he plans to look for a different job based on his own personal desire for more collaboration, more problem solving, more creativity, and more design — and less isolation, less nitty-gritty detail, less uncertainty, stagnation, and routine. These are Jason's career ingredients — some to include, and some to exclude.

Another one of my clients, Antonio, wanted to put down roots in Toronto but didn't want to be tethered to a job that would limit his ability to travel. He has parents in Europe, a sister on the West Coast, and a brother in New York. It's important to him that he be able to visit them for more than two weeks a year.

Antonio also wanted to work in the arts and had a particular passion for arts festivals. He decided to build a career that combined a series of festival contracts with a web design business on the side. The time in between festival contracts would allow him to travel and see his family, and the web design business would provide some financial stability during those periods. He would take on more clients as needed.

This particular career plan may appeal to you, or it may send you running for the hills. But the important thing is that it's a perfect fit for *Antonio*. It includes all of the career ingredients he wanted more of (arts, festivals, freedom to travel, financial stability, variety) and none of the ones he wanted less of (corporate work, a rigid vacation schedule).

What ingredients do *you* want more of in your career? What are the things you already love, and what would you love to add?

More autonomy? More travel? A friendlier corporate culture? More structure and direction? More transparency? More variety? More routine? More mentorship? More teamwork? Clear, detailed processes? Something more entrepreneurial?

What career ingredients do you want less of? What are the aspects of your work you don't like?

Figuring out what you *don't* want can be one of the most helpful tools in figuring out what you *do* want.

Report writing? Meetings? Commuting? Bureaucracy? Shift work? Nights and weekends at the office? Research? Rigid processes? A hectic, cluttered work environment?

Oddly enough, figuring out what you *don't* want can be one of the most helpful tools in figuring out what you *do* want — because for most people, it's easier to start there. Rule out anything that contains too many of the ingredients that turn you off. No job is perfect, but the parts you don't like should be the exceptions, not the norm.

Consider the many ways that you could combine your career ingredients into your own unique career. You don't have to commit to a single one of these combinations. You're just exploring the possibilities, embracing your inner Iron Chef. Some of the most unique and delicious combinations come together when there is no exact recipe. That's true in the kitchen, and it can be true for your career, too.

I CAN'T
WORK IN THESE CONDITIONS!

You would not believe how many workspaces I scoped out before I finally decided on one. I'm not an especially picky person, but I am very sensitive to my physical environment. Always have been. Too noisy? Forget it. Too cluttered? Stress! Too stark or sterile? Ew, how uninspiring. When it comes to my workspace, it has to look and feel a certain way.

I like my space to feel like a hug — warm, welcoming, and calming — with a touch of nature. Gimme some exposed brick, some unfinished wood, good light, lots of plants, and a big plush chair, and I'm a happy camper. I'm a better coach, better writer, better businesswoman — better everything — in that space.

Get me in the wrong space, and I'm frustrated, brain-fried, and distracted. But get me in the right space, and it's like MAGIC. Why? Because my physical environment happens to be one of the most important ingredients for creating my ideal work conditions. In choosing the right space, I'm creating conditions for successful work. The right conditions can raise the quality of your work and elevate your level of happiness and fulfillment — and physical environment is just the tip of the iceberg.

The right conditions can raise the quality of your work and elevate your level of happiness and fulfillment.

Consider your work schedule in your current job. Even if you work a rigid nine-to-five schedule, you probably have some autonomy in how you split up your work tasks, how you group various work activities, and how you manage your time. I only recently discovered my ideal work schedule, and it has made a huge difference. I don't like task switching. I like to work long and deep, so I schedule long stretches of time doing one activity. That lets me get in the zone. Some people prefer the opposite. They like to switch things up and keep everything fresh. Your schedule is definitely one of the ways you can create ideal conditions for successful work.

What about your ideal level of interaction at work? How much do you like connecting with and working with others? A little or a lot? And how many people do you like working with at once? These questions largely depend on your level of extraversion.

I'm extremely introverted, so I manage my time with others very carefully. Large groups (hell, even small groups) are just not my thing. In fact, I find them exhausting. If I'm speaking at a conference, I'll take regular "recharge" breaks by finding a quiet place to walk or sit by myself before joining the crowd again.

I prefer interacting with people one-on-one, which is why I do individual coaching instead of group coaching. That intimacy is important to me. Even so, I schedule at least 30 minutes of quiet "me time" (checking email, writing, farting around on Facebook) in between each of my appointments with clients. It helps me recharge and refocus my energy, so I can be fully present for the next person I'm working with.

Something as simple as choosing to work with digital versus analog tools might also play a part in creating your ideal conditions for successful work. Many of us are hunched over our computers and phones all day, but there are often opportunities to kick it old school with pen and paper. Sometimes switching from digital to analog makes your work drastically better — not to mention refreshing and more enjoyable.

Most of my writing (including this) is scribbled in a little notebook before it ever gets published. I do too much editing and self-censorship when I write directly into my MacBook. Paper and pen feels less restrictive. I can be messy. I think more creatively. I've heard similar remarks from graphic designers who prefer to sketch on paper before using software, and from business professionals working on everything from proposals to copywriting to event planning — people who say they think more creatively when they're sitting with a writing instrument and a blank page. Haven't stepped away from your screen in a while? Give it a whirl.

Other things to consider when you're thinking about creating your ideal work conditions: Do you like to work with your hands? Do you want to make something? Be creative? Indoors or outdoors? Use your imagination? Use logic? Problem solve? Help others? In what way?

How much structure do you like? How important is flexibility to you? What kind of people do you like to work with? Do you like novelty or routine? How do you feel about commuting? Working from home? Do you like mental work or physical work or a combination of both? What kind of office culture do you like? Do you want to work for a big company or a small one? A start-up or your own business?

How important is salary? Commission? Benefits? Security? Mentorship? Creative freedom? Flexibility? The list goes on and on and on.

Of course, the notion of creating ideal conditions for success can extend beyond your work life and into your personal life, too. Take health, for example. A lot of people love going to the gym. Not me. Put me on a treadmill, and I'll throw a raging fit, but a long walk in nature? Giddy up! For me, nature is an important component of physical health. For you, it might be adventure, or mindfulness, or team sports. To each his own.

And cooking! Some people are meal magicians. I am not one of those people. I'm impatient and easily frustrated. I have a terrible habit of trying to cook when I'm already starving and I have no ingredients to work with. When I realize I can't MacGyver a meal together out of week-old asparagus and a tube of toothpaste, I get all stabby. I'm like King Kong in the kitchen.

To create the right conditions for success in the kitchen, I need a plan and the right ingredients on hand, which is why I started creating a weekly menu and matching grocery list (therefore creating my ideal conditions for success). Things are so much easier now. I'm no longer thrashing angrily when I try to cook.

The takeaway? Getting clear on the right conditions for your career can mean the difference between a happy camper and, well, King Kong — whether it's in the kitchen or at work.

HOT
AND COLD

A lot of people have trouble figuring out what they want to do with their career. Sure, you can think up a long list of potential careers, but how in the hell are you supposed to know which one is the best fit, right?

As a result, there are an awful lot of people out there who are just waiting for their ideal career calling to be magically revealed to them. Maybe you're one of them. You're standing there, shuffling your feet, waiting to be struck by lightning, at which point you'll exclaim, *Eureka! THIS is exactly what I should do!* Then you'll ride off into the sunset, certain of your destiny, with a detailed plan of how to make all your wildest dreams come true.

Oh, honey, it *sooooo* doesn't work that way.

Lightning strikes are offered to a lucky few, and the rest of us poor suckers simply have to roll up our sleeves and figure it out ourselves. The universe does not offer exact GPS coordinates.

Pursuing your ideal career is more like playing a game of hot and cold. If you turn away from the things that feel cold and toward the things that feel warmer, you *will* get there.

If you feel defeated by this career path stuff, or if your frustration with it is boiling into a rage, consider this: You're not supposed to know exactly what it looks like.

You're not supposed to know exactly what it looks like.

Perhaps this comes as a surprise to you. A lot of people beat themselves up because they think they're supposed to know exactly what their ideal career looks like. So they refuse to experiment with or commit to even minor changes until they know what the big picture will look like in exacting detail. Then, and only then, will they give themselves permission to move forward.

But that's not how it works. Absolute certainty with a satisfaction guarantee never comes — in your career or in the rest of your life — and in the meantime, you've

The
universe
does not
offer exact
GPS
coordinates.

locked your feet in blocks of cement. If you're not willing to commit to something, you need to at least be willing to *experiment* with something. The alternative means choosing an inert life by default.

Don't let your fear of uncertainty or your need for control paralyze you. Instead, build trial and error into the process. Use what you *do* know, and start learning more. Do some research. The internet has more to offer than just cat videos! Get to know more about different industries. Read about them. And talk to the people in them.

Maybe you think you'd like to do freelance design work. Ask a couple of people who do that out for coffee. What is their day like? How did they get started? What are their challenges? Gather information.

Maybe you think you'd like to start your own photography business. To begin with, take a single class in business or in photography — or both. See what you can learn.

Maybe you think you'd like to go to nursing school. Talk to your aunt who's a nurse. Ask her to fill you in and give it to you straight. Meet with someone in the admissions office at the nursing school. Find out what you need to get in. Ask about the program structure, cost, and time demands.

This is often how discovering a feel-good career happens — not by waiting, but by doing. Learning. Exploring. Hot. Cold. Hot. Cold. That's how Goldilocks did it, and you know what? She was onto something. Eventually you'll find something that is just right.

MORE HAPPY
OR LESS HAPPY?

I was on Instagram the other day, not posting anything or looking for anything in particular. I was just mindlessly scrolling through my feed without even really noticing what I was seeing. I zoned out like this for a couple of minutes (or half an hour . . . who knows?) and then I thought, *Why am I even doing this? It's not even fun.*

I love Instagram — and Twitter, and Facebook! But sometimes they're just kind of a time suck — the places where I go when I'm avoiding something else, like actually doing my work, or making eye contact with strangers in the elevator. I go there to numb out.

I have a friend who says the same thing about Netflix. She'll zone out and binge-watch three or four hours after work every night to dull the boredom/stress/ailment of the day.

The thing is, numbing out doesn't actually feel all that good in the long run. It just feels less bad. And only temporarily. Talk about setting the bar low.

Ever sit down with a bag of cookies and suddenly realize you've eaten six without really noticing? (Or is it just me?) That's why I can't keep cookies in the house. They're the first thing I turn to when I'm stressed or bored or avoiding something. It's just another way to numb out. I know I'm not alone.

Is this making me more happy or less happy?

Now there's nothing wrong with social media, or Netflix, or cookies. Those things are effing *delightful*. The problem is how we (and I include myself here) sometimes use them — as a numbing agent for stress, boredom, and avoidance.

So I've started asking myself, *Is this making me more happy or less happy?*

Zoning out on Instagram that day was making me feel

less happy, but when I use it with intention — whether it's to post something or see what people are up to — it makes me more happy. Mindlessly wolfing down six cookies on a stress binge? Less happy. Enjoying one or two as a fun little treat? More happy. Numbing out with hours and hours of Netflix every night? Less happy. Planning a viewing party when the new season of *House of Cards* comes out? More happy.

Is this making me more happy or less happy? You can ask yourself this question when you notice yourself numbing out, but how about applying it more broadly? Like to your career.

Think about the last time you had a late night at the office. Did it make you more happy or less happy? You may find the answer to this question is, *It depends.* If you were burning the midnight oil for a fulfilling project that was in the home stretch, it might have actually made you *more* happy. That kind of thing can feel exhilarating and empowering when it happens occasionally, but if it's the norm you may be slowly working your way to burnout. *Less* happy.

So what? you might be thinking. *Some stuff in my career makes me feel less happy. What am I supposed to do? Just say fuck it and hang out at the zoo all day?*

Not quite.

Ditch your job for the zoo if you must (hopefully you are also independently wealthy), but sometimes we make tough choices in the interest of *future* happiness.

I have a client who is building her own business. After more than 20 years, she doesn't dig her industry anymore, so she's changing career paths radically and building something of her own. But she didn't quit her job. Not yet. She doesn't plan to quit for another year or two. She'd rather stick it out at her less-than-ideal gig in the interest of providing more stability for her future business. She'll have more savings and less pressure. More happiness later.

Another client of mine made the opposite decision. She felt like her job was crushing her soul and sapping her energy, leaving her little opportunity to work on her biz on the side. She had a lot of hustle and heart (and a decent financial cushion), so she just up and quit. Sure, she could have had *more* of a financial cushion if she'd stuck it out for a while, but for her the best decision was ripping off the Band-Aid. Instant gratification. More happiness now.

Often the question becomes, *Is the short-term pain worth the long-term gain?* Sometimes yes. Sometimes no. Only you know.

In a different scenario, the question might be, *Is the short-term gain worth the long-term pain?* Think back to the cookies. Scarfing a bunch of garbage food might feel kind of nice in the moment (short-term gain), but doing that over and over is going to start to feel shitty (long-term pain).

Happy now or happy later — it doesn't always have to be one or the other. What if you could have *both*?

Rachel is another client of mine who is starting her

own business. She doesn't have a very big financial cushion to make the transition to working on the business full-time, but, on the other hand, her job leaves her exhausted and stressed out, with little time or energy to work on the business on evenings or weekends. What's a gal to do? Stay in her job and burn out, or quit and hope her business is a smashing success right out of the gate?

Neither.

Rachel just left her old job and took a new one so that she can slowly build a solid foundation for her business *and* stay sane while doing so. Win-win. She didn't have to choose between happiness now and happiness later.

My point? There is no one-size-fits-all answer. What works for Rachel, or me, or your best friend might not work for you. The important thing is to ask yourself the right questions. Is what you're doing making you more happy or less happy? When you're faced with a tough decision, do you go for more happiness now or more happiness later? And most importantly — do you really have to choose?

YOU
DO YOU

What's the mark of an adventure seeker?

Scars. Scars are literally the marks of adventure seekers.

I have a scar. It's about two inches long, and it's on the top of my left foot. *Rock climbing accident?* you ask. *Scraped it snorkeling in the Great Barrier Reef? Cliff-diving injury?*

Nope.

I slipped and fell. At the fucking spa. I was oily from my massage, and I slipped on the pool deck.

Hardcore, I'm not. I've never been a big adventure seeker. My idea of a fun time is a night in by myself with a good book (or, evidently, a day at the spa).

Some people might think that's lame. I could be out

doing exciting things! Things like rock climbing and snorkeling and cliff diving! But you know what? That's not my jam. Books are. And sweatpants.

You love what you love. It might not be glamorous or full of adventure (or maybe it is!), but who cares?

You do you.

It's like that with work, too.

I have a client, Gianna, who works in public relations and hates it. I asked her to recall a time when she felt really engaged in her work. She said it was when she was studying for the GMAT for her MBA.

Gianna easily stepped into a leadership role with her MBA classmates, but she wouldn't take the wheel in her public relations career. She hates the pressure of being creative. It's not her strong suit, and she finds it exhausting. She works best when she's working within specific parameters. Constraints bring out her best work.

She loves math, logic, problem solving, numbers, rationality, and using rules to make order out of something. She doesn't get to use *any* of that in her P.R. work, so she's making a radical change and becoming — can you guess? — an accountant.

Her P.R. job — a gig she hated — might have been someone else's dream job (in fact, I *know* it is), but it wasn't Gianna's dream job. "Won't people think I'm crazy for leaving a so-called glamorous job to become an accountant?" she wondered.

Answer: Yes.

But fear of judgment is no reason to stay in a job you hate. If accounting lights you up, *own* it! What would we do without our accountants?! Same goes for our insurance agents, mortgage underwriters, and financial advisors. We need these people. It may not be traditionally glamorous work, but thank goodness there are people who love it and are super amazing at it.

A client of mine is so jazzed about the elegance of Excel spreadsheets that she spends her free time learning from Excel mentors and teaching herself more about it off the clock. That's not exactly on everybody's hit list, but she loves it.

There are no bad jobs — just bad fits.

My lawyer does paperwork all day. And you know what? That guy is a fucking *rock star*. He exudes positive energy. That kind of work would bring me to tears, but he's right in his element, kicking ass and getting shit done every day and *loving* it.

There are no bad jobs — just bad fits.

Be warned: Once you discover what the *right* fit is,

the backpedaling and second-guessing will commence. There's nothing like getting one step closer to happiness to make you FREAK OUT and talk yourself out of actually embracing it. It's a fear response, and it happens to so many people.

"But I'm not really good at P.R.," Gianna said. "Maybe that's a useful skill to learn. Maybe I should stick with it."

Here's what that rationalization sounds like: *Maybe I should stick it out with this thing I hate instead of using my natural gifts in a way that would make me happy*. That's just crazy. Not to mention miserable.

I'm all for growth, but not in a direction that feels bad. Flex the muscle you have and build in other areas when you *want* to, not because you think you *have* to. Big difference.

Sometimes the quest for improvement distracts us from using our innate talents. It's a shame to ignore your natural gifts and interests in favor of filling your gaps. Use your gifts. Do something with them that will make you happy. It's shocking how often we need encouragement to do this. We forget ourselves in the scramble to get better, be better, and do more.

Where do you feel most like yourself? Where do you get to use your natural gifts and talents? Where do you feel like you lose track of time? The answers to these questions are *massive* career clues. Who cares if the work isn't prestigious or glamorous? You love what you love, so go ahead and love it.

What other people think isn't worth the hype, and I'm sorry to be the one to break it to you, but people think about you and your career a lot less than you think they do. They're too busy worrying about what everybody else thinks of *them*.

When you do you, it doesn't matter what other people think. Because you're out there kicking ass and doing shit you love. It's *your* life. Live it up.

EMBRACE
YOUR INNER MOLLY RINGWALD

Remember Molly Ringwald? The '80s teen icon from the movies *Sixteen Candles*, *Pretty in Pink*, and *The Breakfast Club*? We know her from the movies, but if you were to ask her what her first love was, she'd say it was music, especially jazz — not acting. In fact, she performed on her first jazz album at the age of six — way before she established an acting career. Oh, and she's also a novelist. *And* an advice columnist.

Basically, Molly Ringwald has taken life by the balls and is doing whatever she damn well pleases. Because who says you have to be just one thing?

Molly Ringwood is a Renaissance woman — a modern Leonardo da Vinci. You probably know da Vinci as an artist, but did you know he was also an engineer, a mathematician, a writer, a scientist, and an inventor? That's pretty badass, if you ask me. Molly Ringwald and Leonardo da Vinci are two examples of people who have created what I call a *collage career* — a career in which you pull together various interests rather than limit yourself to just one thing. I see more and more people — my friends, colleagues, and clients — crafting their very own unique collage careers as they go.

My friend Lisa loves decorating cakes. She's completing a Ph.D. at a business school and plans to be a full-time professor one day, but she also has a side business making cakes. She's proud of her creations and posts photos of her masterpieces on Facebook. She didn't go to school for it. She's not making a bunch of money from it. But she loves it, so she's made room for it in her life.

One of my clients, Miranda, is obsessed with film, specifically cinematography. She wouldn't let herself indulge in this fascination until very recently; it wasn't practical. What good would come of it? I encouraged her to indulge anyway. She began attending film discussion groups and started her own film appreciation blog. In doing so, she's building a community of other film enthusiasts. She's even considering taking a film course, but she's in no rush. One thing at a time.

My partner, Phil, is a theater nut. It doesn't pay the bills for him, but he's found a way to make it a part of his life's work. He also works for a progressive start-up.

He has flexible work hours, and his employer accommodates his requests for time off to produce and perform in shows. Flexibility and accommodation were two of Phil's most important career ingredients. He found a gig that had them, and he's written, directed, and acted in four shows this year thanks to it.

These people are indulging their passions, fascinations, and curiosities. None of them waited until they knew how to make these things pay off the mortgage before they started. Because who knows if they ever will? Knowing isn't the point. Inviting the things you love to be a bigger part of your life is the point. Maybe it will eventually lead to a paycheck. Maybe it will be a really rewarding passion project. You won't know until you're willing to dabble a little bit. And, let me tell you, dabbling is *essential*.

But dabbling sounds frivolous and silly, right? Even the word sounds wishy-washy. Still, I've found that dabbling is really and truly the only way to test the waters before diving in. It's a way to see if something you *think* you might like is something you *actually* like — because your idea of something and the reality of it may be two very different things. You have to try it on first, take it for a test-drive, kick the tires.

Knowing isn't the point.

And if you have no idea what you like, the best thing to do is dabble with the things you're curious about. Passion begins as curiosity. Anyone who is passionate about something was curious about it first. You have to learn more, lean in to it, and give it a try — that's the alchemy of transforming curiosity into passion.

If you're not willing to try anything new or to return to the things you once loved, how can you expect to just *know* what you like? Passion isn't just going to land in your lap. Not without an invitation.

So dabble with the things that fascinate you. And if you don't know what those things are, follow your curiosities. There may be no paycheck (maybe not right away, at least), but I guarantee there will be a payoff.

Passion begins as curiosity.

THE
RESISTANCE

YOU COULD SPEND YOUR WHOLE LIFE
DELIBERATING INSTEAD OF DOING.

JUST
GIMME A SIGN

YOU: *Universe, please send me a sign.*

UNIVERSE: *Dude, start paying attention.*

I have a client, Ava, who loved to make her own homemade salad dressings at the age of eight. Salad dressings. At the age of eight. While other kids were playing with Polly Pockets and Pokémon, she was mixing oils and vinegars and herbs. How many eight-year-olds do you know who love to do that?

To this day, Ava loves making her own healthy recipes, trying different flavors, and sharing her knowledge with others. She loves helping people use food as a way to feel good. She does this on her own time and is generous with her knowledge.

Ava is also fascinated with holistic health and wellness. She can't learn enough about it. In one conversation, she listed six or seven wellness practitioners she works with — acupuncturist, craniosacral therapist, naturopathic doctor, nutritionist, dietitian . . . the list goes on. She loves learning from these wellness experts.

Any idea what Ava should be doing with her career?

Of course you do. She's on a path to work in holistic wellness.

> *Everybody* has the intuition muscle. For many, it's just atrophied from lack of use.

This was an obvious choice for her, right? Wrong. It was a struggle to get there. She didn't see all of the signs.

"I'm not very self-aware," she said. "I don't have very good intuition."

I get this from clients all the time. My response? "Well then, let's start working that muscle."

Because *everybody* has the intuition muscle. For many,

it's just atrophied from lack of use. That muscle is fully functioning in childhood, by the way. Kids play what they want to play (even the salad dressing game), and they do so with reckless abandon. They're highly focused, fully engaged, and they don't second-guess themselves.

Most of us lose that focus and engagement and confidence as we grow up. We learn more about *rules* and unlearn much of what we know *intuitively*. That's why remembering what you loved when you were a child can be such a good career clue; we still followed our intuition back then.

But if you unlearn what you know intuitively, you start ignoring your hunches; and if you ignore your hunches for long enough, you don't even notice them anymore. It's like slowly fashioning your own psychological blinders. You can't see the big picture anymore. You can't connect the dots.

Luckily the dots are there. And findable.

Remembering what you used to love helps. We've already explored that. Noticing what your body is trying to tell you also helps. For example, Ava's face lit up when we talked about the possibility of a career in holistic wellness. Her eyes opened wider, she sat up straighter, she leaned forward. This was her body's way of saying, *OMG yes!*

We also talked about the possibility of her becoming a naturopathic doctor. Her shoulders hunched, she slumped back in her seat, and her face fell. She looked deflated. This was also a sign.

"Your body language says this is a no," I said. "Is that right?" It was. Naturopathic medicine was too technical and all that schooling felt too cumbersome for Ava. Holistic wellness is what she was really jazzed about.

All of the signs pointed to this — signs from her hobbies and passions, signs from her childhood, and even signs from her body — but Ava still second-guessed what she knew intuitively. As most of us do.

Like many of the people I work with, Ava told me that she really wanted to keep going down this particular path, but she was afraid there was some other option she wasn't considering.

My response: Yes. Yes, there is. There are *lots* of options you aren't considering. Because you are not being called to do any of that other stuff.

But how will I be 100 percent sure
this path is right for me?!

ANSWER: You won't. Not ever.

You could spend your whole life deliberating instead of doing. But at some point you have to put your desire to pursue one path ahead of your need for certainty and your fear of making a mistake. For some people, a certain career calling feels so strong that it cannot be ignored. For others, it takes a bit of work to get there. You have to notice the signs and surrender to what they tell you.

If all of the signs are pointing in one direction — then for the love of god, don't fight it.

Don't fight your intuition. It's the best tool you have. When you ignore the signs, muffle your intuition, and disregard your hunches, it's not uncertainty that's stopping you from moving forward; it's fear in the form of willful ignorance.

The need to examine every possible option doesn't just slow things down, it's paralyzing. Your need for absolute certainty is not prudent, it's not pragmatic — it's crippling.

My advice? Admit what you know intuitively. Notice the signs. Follow your hunches. They know the way.

> Your need for absolute certainty
> is not prudent, it's not pragmatic
> — it's crippling.

YOU CAN'T
QUARANTINE DESIRE

I can remember the first time I let my guard down at the beginning of a romantic relationship. I'm rarely the first to show my cards, but after a really great first date I took a deep breath and sent a message: "I'm really into you. I'd like to see you again. I can't remember the last time I connected with someone in this way." It felt incredibly freeing to express how I felt.

That feeling lasted for exactly 30 seconds before it was washed away by a hot wave of panic — a mix of frantic uncertainty and searing regret. I was now susceptible to being hurt — the very definition of vulnerability.

In one of her TED talks, Dr. Brené Brown calls this post-exposure feeling of regret and dread a "vulnerability hangover." It's the perfect term because it captures the euphoric high of being completely open paired with a subsequent crash of anxiety.

It takes guts to go after something. So why do we do it?

Because if you keep yourself closed off, you never actually get what you want. That includes what you want for your career.

Whether it's making amends with a colleague, asking for a raise, requesting help, admitting you don't understand, going for the promotion, starting your own business, or making a career change, good things can happen when you take down your walls. Bad things can happen, too. And, yes, there is the risk of disappointment.

The prevailing thought is that if you don't put yourself out there, you can't get hurt. Wrong. You're hurting yourself every time you refuse to go after what you want.

Some will say that by wearing your heart on your sleeve, you relinquish the power of cool. You're out there on a limb, naked and exposed. Maybe so, but if you don't put yourself out there, people won't know what you want. Playing it cool is overrated. So is playing it safe.

Playing it safe means keeping a long, safe distance between yourself and what you want. There's no risk of disappointment or defeat if you never actually try to do the thing you've been called to do. What there is — and you won't see this until years down the road — is regret. I haven't worked with a single person in their 50s or 60s who hasn't expressed regret over not going after what they wanted sooner.

You can't quarantine desire. You can ignore it. You can tune it out. You can refuse to face it. But desire cannot be sequestered, sealed off, or banished. You carry your calling with you.

Songbirds answer a specific call. Chickadees are named for their chipper, repetitive *chicka-dee-dee-dee* call. Mourning doves answer a melancholy, lilting call. Red-winged blackbirds answer an electronic-ish call that, weirdly, sounds a lot like old school dial-up internet.

You can't quarantine desire. You can ignore it. You can tune it out. You can refuse to face it. But desire cannot be sequestered, sealed off, or banished. You carry your calling with you.

When a songbird is trying to unite with his peeps (like, say, when he's looking for an attractive mate), he sends out a specific call and hopes for a response from one of his own.

It's like that with careers, too. You feel compelled to do

something because you hear the call. You don't hear every calling. Just yours. There are thousands and thousands of callings you don't hear because they're not for you. You're tuned in to a very specific frequency and feel called to do a very few specific things. Coincidence? Nope.

You will continue to hear your calling until you answer it. It's in your nature, in your DNA, a part of survival — for your soul, if not also for your mind and body.

One of my favorite quotes from the poet/scholar Rumi is "What you seek is seeking you." That's what a calling is. You are both seeking and being sought.

To refuse the call is to place an embargo on your own happiness, to seal it off and place it out of bounds. This is like tenderly wrapping your heart in barbed wire. Sure, nothing can get in, but you're only hurting yourself.

Answering your calling, despite the excruciating vulnerability required to do so — not to mention the certainty of making mistakes along the way — is the surest bet for a happy life. Because making a few mistakes is infinitely better than never knowing, and the ache of disappointment is not nearly as painful as the unanswered yearning.

WELCOME
TO THE RESISTANCE

Let's say you find the guts to actually tune in to your calling. Then what? This is the part where you take a deep, steely breath and go for it with fierce determination, riding off into the sunset, right?

Nope.

Hell nope.

This is the part where every fiber of your being tries to throw you off course, hammer on the brakes, and sabotage all of your efforts. Welcome to the resistance. This is when you try to busy yourself with other important things (and also many unimportant things) in order to avoid doing the one thing you're terrified of doing, even though you desperately want to do it.

How do I know this? Experience, baby.

I recently designed an online course for aspiring career changers. I loved that project with my whole heart and soul. I felt called to do it. And yet I fought it. *Hard*. I busied myself with other things. Even when I set aside time to develop the course, I found every excuse and opportunity to stray from it. For example, here are some things I did to avoid working on the course. This is just in ONE DAY:

- Gave myself a pedicure.
- Watched last week's episode of *The Bachelor*.
- Facebooked.
- Had a bowl of Cap'n Crunch.
- Stared into the open refrigerator.
- Made guacamole.
- Ate entire batch of said guacamole.
- Made brownies. (Do you see a theme developing here?)
- Went on a Starbucks run.
- Bought another new notebook.
- Filed new notebook with several other unused notebooks.
- Checked email every five minutes.
- Watched a video of a wild gorilla reunited with the man who raised him.
- Googled "how many calories are in an entire pan of brownies."

- Organized my closet.
- Watched a TED video.
- Watched five more TED videos.
- Bought 12 domain names I'll probably never use.
- Took nine photos of my cat. Instagrammed one.
- Started a new project.
- Tidied my desktop.
- Found 14 abandoned new projects on my desktop.
- Checked my bank balance.
- Read yesterday's paper.
- Filled my cart at katespade.com. Actually bought nothing.
- Made a to do list (because there's nothing like making a list of the shit you need to do instead of actually doing it).

My point? I know just as well as the next person exactly what it feels like to actively and persistently resist something you want.

In *The War of Art: Break Through the Blocks and Win Your Inner Creative Battles*, author Steven Pressfield says, "The more important a call or action is to our soul's evolution, the more Resistance we will feel toward pursuing it." That's absolutely been true for me, and it's true for the people I work with, as well.

We often resist what we desire most. Why? Because the stakes are so damn high, that's why. We're terrified that if we actually go for it, we'll fuck it up. *What if I suck at this? What if people think I'm an idiot? What if I change my mind? What if I fail?*

Resistance is just one big chronic case of the *what ifs*. And the *what ifs* are paralyzing.

So what's a person caught in the grip of resistance to do? First, notice the resistance. Second, call its bluff. You'll have to say things like:

> *Listen, Resistance, I know it's technically possible that we've received a life-changing email in the past five minutes, but frankly the chances are slim. How about we try to work for just 30 minutes, and then we can have an email break? M'kay?*

OR

> *Hey, Resistance, that looks like a delicious batch of brownies you've whipped up there, but didn't you just scarf a whole batch of guacamole? I think you're trying to avoid working on that scary thing you want to do. Step away from the baked goods. Back away slowly.*

OR

> *Whatcha doin' there, Resistance? Scrubbing the toilet? Doing your taxes? Going shopping?*

Watching internet cat videos? Cleaning the fridge? Rearranging your closet? Checking the score of last night's game? Watching old Seinfeld *reruns? All of those things are very nice, but is it important that you do them right now, or are you avoiding something?*

When you're doing shit like this, you *are* avoiding something. And while your little buddy, Resistance, is trying to spare you discomfort, he's also crippling you before you even get started.

First, notice the resistance. Second, call its bluff.

Moving through resistance is like playing a game of Red Light, Green Light. It happens in short, choppy bursts. Just as you get going, you'll come halting to a stop. Then you'll feel safe taking a few steps forward. Until you don't. And this whole cycle will repeat itself until you're at your destination. Getting there doesn't require that you conquer your fear or proceed in one fluid motion, just that you move through your resistance, choppy and spastic as it is.

Give it a whirl. And, hey, if you try and fail, I've got brownies.

EXCUSES,
EXCUSES

One of my clients, Wendy, sat on an idea for a gourmet cake business for more than 20 years. *Twenty* years! Back then, she thought she was too inexperienced. More recently, she wondered if maybe she was too old. Now, armed with a business plan and a kick in the pants from yours truly, Wendy is well on her way with that cake business.

My mom was never a whiz with electronics. She could run a farm business, fix a sewing machine, drive a tractor, and cook a delicious meal for seven, but ask her to use the remote control or email an attachment, and she was lost.

My mother now runs a thriving business selling hand-made children's clothing. She can hardly keep up with her orders. Did I mention it's an *online* business? Mom taught herself everything she needed to know to make it happen. Part of me is shocked, and part of me isn't a bit surprised. When I visit my parents, one of my favorite things to see is Mom curled up with her laptop in sweats and Crocs, glasses perched on the tip of her nose as she checks her orders headed for Japan and Australia. It's pretty damn cool.

A client, April, wanted to write for major publications as a way to gain exposure and credibility for her new business. "But I can't do that," she said. "I'm so new to this. I mean, who the hell do I think I am?" I reminded her that every writer there ever was started by publishing just one thing and then building from there. In less than a year, she was published at *Inc.*, *Business Insider*, and *Forbes*. Not too shabby.

April could have decided that writing for major business publications while she was still a rookie was too big of a stretch.

My mom could have decided that she couldn't run an online business because she didn't know computers.

Wendy could have decided that it was simply too late to try to get that gourmet cake business off the ground.

What excuses are *you* making for not going after what you want? And do they really have to stop you?

A colleague of mine wants to work as a strategy consultant. He has a master's degree from a great business school and is whip-smart.

"But I'm too young," he said. "Nobody will take me seriously. Plus, I don't have much experience."

"But couldn't you get experience by working under a mentor?" I asked.

"I guess so," he said. "But people will never take me seriously. I'm just too young."

A few weeks later, I had a conversation with a senior business executive. His company had restructured, and suddenly he was out of work.

"I've always wanted to work as a consultant," he said. "I guess I could try that, but I'm too old. People will think I'm out of touch."

There is no magic age to work as a consultant. Or a lawyer. Or a chef. Or a designer. Or a yoga instructor. Or a gymnast. Okay, maybe there is a magic age to work as a gymnast (15?), but you get my point.

Nor is there a magic weight, background, look, hair color, height, or shoe size.

The following are actual excuses I've heard from people for not going after what they want:

- I'm too young. Nobody will take me seriously.
- I'm too old. People will think I'm out of touch.
- I have a thick accent. I can't do a podcast.
- I'm a bad dresser. I'll look uncool on camera.
- I'm too fat for TV.
- My butt is too big to do public speaking.
- I'm not creative enough to write good sales copy.

- I can't put a photo on my website. I have terrible teeth.
- I'm dyslexic. I can't start my own business.
- I can't teach. I have a stutter.
- I'm not the best writer. I can't start a blog.
- I'm too shy. I could never make it in sales.
- I'm not rich. I can't open my own shop.
- I can't get my master's degree. I've been out of school for too long.
- I'm a single mother. I can't take a class.
- I can't show people my spiritual side. It will turn them off.
- I live in a small town. I won't get clients.
- I don't have a degree in that. I'll have no credibility.

Notice how the things on this list follow a predictable formula:

I'm too _____ to do that.

I'm not _____ enough to do that.

Are you walking around with some similar assumptions? If so, I can almost guarantee that your assumptions are preventing you from going after what you want.

What excuses are you walking around with? Fill in the blanks.

I'm too _____ to

_____.

I'm not _____ enough to

_____.

How true is this story you're telling yourself? Are these things real obstacles, or do they sound more like excuses? Know the difference.

What excuses are you walking around with?

I'M FINE,
REALLY'

If you've really invested in your excuses, and their hold on you feels too strong, you may have let them break you down to the point of resignation. *I obviously can't have what I want, so I'm just going to settle for this. I'm okay with it. I'm fine, really.*

Bullshit.

If that were true, you wouldn't be reading this.

Maybe you've resigned yourself to doing work you hate because it looks good from the outside. Maybe you have an enviable gig with prestige, pay, and benefits, but you ask yourself, *Why am I so unhappy?* You tell yourself that you should be happy, and in doing so, you not only feel miserable, but also guilty for feeling that way. So you suck it up. You're fine.

There is no honor in sucking it up — in resigning yourself to something less than you deserve.

If you've resigned yourself to settling for something you don't want, you are not fine. You're discouraged. You've lost hope. And that's not fine. You can silver line the hell out of your problems, but there comes a point at which optimism becomes denial.

There is no honor in sucking it up — in resigning yourself to something less than you deserve.

I'm all for looking on the bright side, but the worst type of spin is spin you try to sell yourself — the stories you weave, trying to convince yourself of one thing or another. You try to make the best of things. You tell yourself, *It's not that bad. Sure, I work 14-hour days at a job I hate and I'm burning out and all of my relationships are falling apart, but shit could be worse.*

Yes, shit could *always* be worse. That's why the status quo is so damn oppressive. You scare yourself into submission with ghost stories about how bad things *could* be. You keep rehearsing the "shit could be worse" story in an effort to drown out another, louder, more obvious truth — shit could be *better*. Way better.

The thing about wanting something better, something more, is it puts you in the hot seat. You're on the hook to actually *do* something about it, and that's a lot of pressure.

So you settle. Because settling is easier. Miserable, but easier. At least at first. The thing about settling is it catches up with you. At some point, the uneasiness grows. What begins as quiet discontent often grows into a deafening call for change. One that can no longer be ignored. Excruciating as that is, it's a good thing. It's what's required to shock us back to life.

What would happen if you stopped saying, *I'm fine, really. Shit could be worse*. Might you have to admit that you want something more and actually do something about it?

Admit the truth.

Notice how it makes you feel.

Do something about it.

BURNOUT, BAGGAGE, & BREAKDOWNS

YOUR BREAKING POINT IS FREEDOM CALLING.

SNAP

Doing too much can be a really sneaky form of avoidance.

Can't you see how busy I am? I literally have ZERO time for frivolities like happiness. It's not even my fault. I'm just the victim here. It's out of my hands.

If this sounds like you, I suggest you put down this book and get back to your busy, miserable life right this second.

Still here? See, you do have time. As much time as everyone else, actually. You just have to own your choices about what you do with it. If that makes you want to flip a table or throw a throat punch in my direction, I get it. I do. I get it because I used to be a victim of time, too. I used to be one giant, raging, seething ball of schedule-induced stress, and all of it — every second — was of my own design.

I remember regularly going off the deep end during a period of my life when I was working my first management job, relocating my department, doubling my staff, and also completing a master's degree during the evenings and weekends. I was frazzled from doing too much and working too hard. I was a short fuse, easily lit and prone to unstable explosions. Anything and everything would launch me into either a fiery rage or a sobbing puddle of self-pity — house-training the puppy, burning dinner, losing my keys . . . you name it. I was either a tear-streaked mess or the Incredible Hulk, often both at once or seconds apart.

During these episodes, I knew how deranged I was acting, yet I felt powerless to stop. I was stretched too thin, and my priorities were out of whack. Everything — from minor issues at work to small annoyances from my husband — was an emergency, an outrage, or a doomsday scenario. (Is it any wonder I got divorced during this period?) I was miserable, exhausted, emotionally unstable, and angry. Losing my keys or burning dinner was never the actual problem. The problem was that I was riding on the back of my beastly, unbridled schedule, living on the edge of unrelenting panic and hanging on for dear life.

Perhaps some of this sounds familiar to you. The weepy meltdowns, the fits of rage, the emotional exhaustion — all of that stuff is partly the product of a stressy, hectic life, but scratch the surface and you're likely to find that something else is wrong, too.

You may find yourself asking, *What's really going on here?* Why the constant distraction? Why the need to create a schedule that pushes me to the brink of insanity? Is there something I don't want to know or deal with?

Maybe you're trying to do too much because you care too much about keeping up with appearances. Maybe you're overextending yourself at work because you don't want to deal with stress at home. Maybe you're feeling lost or unfulfilled, and chaos feels better than emptiness. Maybe you're busy repressing something that deeply needs to be resolved. Maybe you're frustrated or angry with a friend or your spouse or yourself, and you'd rather stay busy than have an uncomfortable confrontation. Maybe you feel uncertain about the future, so you'd rather be consumed by a frantic present. Maybe you're terrified by what you want, so you need a diversion — distraction by any means necessary, even monotony and misery.

Truth often emerges in stillness and silence, and so the blaring discord of a frenetic existence should keep it at bay, right?

Truth often emerges in stillness and silence, and so the blaring discord of a frenetic existence should keep it at bay, right? Sure, but that's no way to live. It doesn't have to be like that. Had anyone mentioned this while I was deep into a rage or pity party, I'd have had to try very hard not to unleash the hounds of hell on their ass. It's hard to see the other side of things when you're at war. But I climbed out of the trenches and made my way to the enemy line, and I'm reporting back: There's nobody out there. The enemy is us. We are only raging against ourselves.

THE
BURNOUT CLUB

Have you ever found yourself so miserable or stressed out at work that you end up getting sick?

There's actually a word for that. Psychoneuroimmunoendocrinology is a field of medicine that deals with the physiological manifestation of psychological stress. In other words, how stress can really mess up your body. It's hard to distill an entire field of medicine (not to mention a 13-syllable word) into a single sentence, but that's it in a nutshell.

Maybe you weren't familiar with the word *psychoneuroimmunoendocrinology* before today (and I swear that's the last time I'll make you read it), but I'd be willing to bet that based only on your personal experience, you know a thing or two about the link between stress and health.

Am I right?

Maybe you battle debilitating exhaustion when you think about making a career change.

Maybe your eczema flares up when you think about applying to grad school. Or quitting grad school.

Maybe you get strep throat like clockwork every time the busy season rolls around and you're overloaded with too much work. Again.

Maybe your digestive system goes haywire when you think about keeping up with the Joneses at your office.

Maybe, like me, your back goes out every time you push yourself to the limit.

Complete the following sentence:

I always get sick or injured when I _____.

Dude, I hear you.

My back is a barometer for my mental health. It used to go out all the time — when I was stressed with a deadline or working too hard on a big proposal, or when I took on too much or had a particularly crazy month. I remember giving my ex-husband a gift certificate for us to go to a rock-climbing gym. His birthday is in October, but we couldn't actually go climbing until February because I had chronic back trouble.

But it wasn't just my back.

For a period of about four years, I saw doctors repeatedly

(with no resolution) for a variety of health problems I just couldn't shake. I had unexplained hives with no apparent allergies. My back went out regularly, immobilizing me for days at a time. I had heavy, debilitating exhaustion and had to nap throughout the day just to function. I woke up in the middle of the night with anxiety attacks. I fainted suddenly while on a subway car and spilled out the doors, face-first, onto a concrete platform.

I was a mess.

I saw doctors, allergists, chiropractors, naturopaths, homeopaths, acupuncturists, and a therapist. I did physiotherapy and rounds of blood work. Once, in desperation, I even traveled hundreds of miles to see a man who I can only describe as a witch doctor. No help. I experienced some temporary relief with some practitioners, but the same issues flared up again and again.

During the same four-year period of chronic illness and injury, I made a radical and terrifying career change, went through a devastating divorce, sold the only home I ever owned, tried to force myself to finish a Ph.D. I hated, lost almost all of my money, and had a personal identity crisis (as tends to happen when there is upheaval in every area of your life).

I am certain that this is not a coincidence.

Stress had basically obliterated my life. I realized there must be a lesson I hadn't learned yet. Unless I wanted to see my life go up in flames again, I had to figure out what it was. And so I combed through the ashes of my former life to look for the lessons.

There were many.

Two of the biggest lessons I learned were:

1. Stop pushing so goddamn hard.
2. Listen to your body.

Why am I sharing all of this personal stuff with you? Because *you* don't have to wait for your life to go up in flames before you learn the lessons. I did it the hard way. You don't have to.

Your body will call your bluff. Every time.

It's easy to rationalize decisions and actions and stuff you think you just *have* to do, especially when it comes to your career. But your body will call your bluff. Every time. It will shut down. It will scream, *Bullshit! Enough! This is not okay. Stop.*

Listen to your body. Before it's too late.

Obviously (but I'm going to go ahead and say it anyway), you should see a doctor for any health-related concerns. Please do that. I don't want an angry letter from some dude who thinks I'm suggesting that deep introspection will heal a bleeding head wound. *Please, sir, stop reading this and dial 911. Thank you. And may you have a speedy recovery.*

But seriously, think of the things that are going on with your physical health, especially any recurring issues. Only you and your doctor can determine what might be causing these symptoms. But if you have an unresolved chronic issue, or recurring health issues, or multiple health issues, don't you think it's possible that some of that is rooted in some neglected stress? Sure, we may feel symptoms of stress even when we make positive changes, but they're usually short-lived, a temporary discomfort — not prolonged health issues stemming from stuff we refuse to address.

Consider what some of your root stressors might be. They may include fear about the future, financial strain, a crappy job, uncertainty, perfectionism, fear of judgment, unhappy relationships, people-pleasing, overanalyzing, working too much, or any number of things.

What is your body trying to tell you? Maybe your body knows that you need to quit your job, or start your own business, or move across the country, or leave your relationship, or have a child, or stop trying so hard to be liked, or do your MBA — or quit your MBA and go to film school instead.

It's very possible that your body knows something that you just don't want to acknowledge. The body doesn't *do* denial. Whatever personal insight you glean from your body, resist the urge to push it back down.

There's nothing more painful than realizing an uncomfortable truth and then trying to repress it. That genie won't go back in the bottle.

Of course, knowing what the problem is and knowing how to fix it are two different things. Figuring out how to fix it will likely take some time. If you know exactly how to make it happen, do it. If not, that's okay. First, you have to connect with your truth. Keep listening. You'll get there.

GUT
CHECK

I know it in the pit of my stomach.

It's a gut decision.

My stomach is in knots.

I finally found the guts to go for it.

We certainly have a lot of phrases linking the gut to decision-making, which is funny because we often think of decision-making as a purely rational process.

But is it, really? And should it be?

The best decisions — including the best career decisions — are made when the gut and the brain work together, with the gut in charge of navigation and the brain in charge of execution.

And I don't just mean gut in the figurative sense. Our bodies give us useful and important information all the time. Often, we don't notice this information — or worse, we disregard it because we live in an age where rationality is king. We worship logic. We operate from the neck up.

We are so disconnected from our bodies.

At any given moment, your body is trying to tell you something. You can choose to ignore it, or you can tap into its wisdom. If that sounds a little too woowoo, hippy dippy for you, think of it as biological feedback. Same thing, different language.

We are so disconnected from our bodies.

One of my mentors, Martha Beck, has a simple exercise that she uses to help people tap into the wisdom of their bodies. She calls it the "body compass." Basically, she'll ask you to recall an unpleasant memory, hold it in your mind, and then notice the sensations you feel in your body, right from your feet to the top of your head. Then she'll ask you to do the same for a positive memory.

My positive memory sensation is a warm tingly feeling on my skin. My negative memory sensation feels like a

don't
wait
until
shit
gets
ugly

suffocating tightening in my throat. I call it the "boa constrictor."

Your own body compass sensations may or may not have anything to do with your actual gut, but for many people, the negative sensation feels like an upset stomach. For others, it's a tension in the shoulders, or a clenching of the jaw, or a tightening in the chest, or, like me, a choking feeling.

Try it yourself. Recall a negative experience. Hold it in your mind. Do a body scan from your toes to the top of your head. What physical sensations do you notice?

Now, do the same for a positive memory.

Martha calls this tool body *compass* and not simply body *scan* because the trick is to use your body sensations to help you navigate the decisions in your life. You should head toward more of the things that make you feel good (warm and tingly, in my case), and away from the things that make you feel bad (that choking boa constrictor feeling).

For me, that boa constrictor sensation is something I feel whenever I force myself to do something I don't really want to do — like fake enthusiasm at a research conference, or hang out with people I don't actually like, or try to do work I hate.

The boa constrictor feeling is like a gentle tap on the shoulder from my body. It's a sign. I should pay attention. When I don't (because who ever listens the first time, right?), I get a big ol' smack upside the head when my back goes out or I get sick.

I have a friend who noticed something interesting once she started paying attention to her body at work. Her manager asked her to cross an ethical boundary with some contracts, and she *literally* got a bad taste in her mouth. *Literally*. She Googled it and it turns out *that's a thing*. Maybe that's where the saying comes from.

When your body offers up information like that, here's what it's saying: *Ummm, this might not be the best idea. May I recommend that you consider a different course of action?*

Ignore it and eventually you'll get a smack upside the head. Your body will start screaming: *I tried to tell you, but you never listen. Can we PLEASE fix this problem now?! Otherwise shit is gonna get ugly.*

My friend, don't wait until shit gets ugly. Notice what you hate. Notice what you love. Stop doing stuff you hate. Start doing stuff you love. Your body will tell you the difference. Every time.

Pay attention.

Correct course as necessary.

Repeat.

SURRENDER

If you've ever found yourself hanging by a very fine thread, you know what it's like to feel a breakdown coming on. It's like watching a tidal wave approach: You can see it coming, but it hasn't yet hit the shore.

A breakdown wins every time. All of the grit and determination in the world aren't enough to fortify yourself against its commanding force. I learned this firsthand after fighting a breakdown during my divorce.

I kicked into overdrive and convinced myself that purchasing furniture for my new apartment was more important than processing what was actually happening. I wasn't going to have a breakdown, I decided; I was going to have a beautifully furnished apartment instead. You can probably guess how that turned out. I had a beautifully furnished apartment. Followed by a breakdown.

Miserable as it was, a breakdown is exactly what I needed to have. A wave of exhaustion washed over me. I slept for days. I sobbed. I rested. I let in a few tried and true friends. Amazingly, once I actually let myself unravel, I felt the fog slowly start to lift.

Breakdowns are damn uncomfortable, but they're cleansing. So if you find yourself on the verge of a breakdown, whether it's related to your career or your personal life, here is my advice: Let it happen. Just surrender.

Like a tidal wave, a breakdown can't be controlled. Trying to keep it at bay is not only futile, but actually prolongs your suffering. Let it wash over you. You'll fear that it will wash you away entirely, but you'll survive. Build yourself a little life raft of support — you'll need time, space, people you trust, and the willingness to endure some pain. It may get worse before it gets better, but it *will* get better.

Having a breakdown is like emergency room triage. You have no choice but to tend to the most serious, life-threatening wounds first. You have to stop the bleeding. That is your first and only priority. Healing and rebuilding will come later.

That's why you can't simply push through and carry on when you're on the cusp of a breakdown. It's about survival. Pushing through and trying to carry on like normal is simply putting off the inevitable. The things we push down catch up with us in time. This I know.

I tried very hard not to have a breakdown when I was waist-deep in academic research. For some, academia feels like a clear blue pool, refreshing and invigorating. For me, that kind of work felt like frigid, black, shark-infested water. Yet I waded deeper and deeper into it, ignoring what I didn't want to know: *This is not where I belong*.

The things we push down catch up with us in time.

Naturally, wading deeper into it while ignoring my truth delivered me right into the belly of the beast — a breakdown. And it happened at the *worst* possible time. I was at a large professional research conference for my field. I was there to present some of my research. I was supposed to do so with enthusiasm, but I couldn't even muster enough interest for polite dinner conversation about my work. A new faculty member asked what I was working on, and I nearly burst into tears right at the table. I didn't want to talk about it. I *hated* conducting research. I hated everything about it, and I certainly didn't want to talk about it at dinner.

Fast forward to two hours later, and I was back in my hotel room having a meltdown. I cried. I cried because I had to. I cried because I was so fucking exhausted from the effort it took *not* to cry. I cried because it was time to really feel it, and time to let go. I finally gave in to my big, messy, inconvenient, unprofessional meltdown.

Oh, and did I mention that I was sharing my hotel room with my colleague Dave, and that he was there when all of this happened? Dave was more of a professional kind of friend, not a witness your snotty-nosed emotional breakdown kind of friend. It was not pretty. Oh well. It happened because it had to. I felt immensely better afterward.

I presented my research the next day, and it took another year (and another breakdown — the Starbucks one) for me to *finally* say farewell to academia. Like I said, the things we push down catch up with us in time. Over and over and over again. Until we *get* it.

So the next time you feel a breakdown coming on, don't fight it. Surrender. Unravel. Rest. Find a soft place to land. Process. It takes strength to address your suffering. But if you let it, the unbearable end of one chapter will spark the beginning of another.

CHECK
YOUR BAGGAGE

WARNING: *I'm about to get all up in your business.*

If you're feeling frustrated, or exhausted, or stuck in your career, maybe it's not your job that's the problem. Maybe it's you.

I may be right, or I may be wrong, but you should at least consider the possibility. A lot of people bring a lot of baggage with them to work. Things like:

- low self-esteem
- workaholism
- control issues
- a need for validation

- perfectionism
- severe anxiety
- bullying
- approval-seeking behavior
- passive-aggressive behavior
- untreated depression
- a constant need to be right
- antagonistic behavior
- overanalyzing
- poor listening skills
- oversensitivity
- unwillingness to compromise
- self-sabotage

What's some of the baggage you carry around with you at work? Try to think of at least three things. They may or may not be on the list above.

You've got to deal with those issues. I say that without judgment. We *all* have issues — you, me, the Dalai Lama, and every other human being on the planet. If this stuff is getting in your way at work (hint: it is), you need to devote some of your energy to doing something about it.

One of my clients, Mona, came to me because she'd had a string of shitty jobs. Nobody appreciated her, and she kept getting let go. She was stuck deep in victim mode when we met. She was also extremely negative. She was negative about everything — her work, her life, her relationships. Even the jokes she made were complaints thinly veiled as humor.

I asked Mona if she thought the problem might be her and not the jobs (which is a pretty ballsy thing to say to someone you've known for 15 minutes). To her credit, Mona took a long, thoughtful pause and said, "Well, shit. Maybe." Later we discovered that she wore her negativity like armor. Nobody could criticize her or her ideas when she was already the world's biggest critic. But Mona's negativity armor was also keeping happiness at bay. She found a way to turn things around, but it took time, self-awareness, practice, and, most importantly, a willingness to get out of her own damn way.

Another client of mine, Anne, liked to turn everything into a crisis. Good things, bad things, and things that didn't even matter at all were framed equally as emergencies, things to worry about and agonize over. This was also a defense mechanism. She thought that hyper-vigilance would prevent anything bad from happening, but in reality, she was missing out on happy moments, ignoring her victories, and wearing herself out in the meantime.

Anne arrived at one of our meetings in a panic because she had received an unexpected job offer out of the blue. She had been trying to discover what kind of career transition she wanted to make, and this job offer had thrown a wrench into the works.

"But I don't know what kind of job I want to do yet!"

"Yes, that's true, but what is it you said you were stressed about last week?"

"Money. I really need to find work soon."

"So why is a job offer landing in your lap a crisis?"

"Because I don't want to have to choose between money and figuring out what I want."

"What makes you think you have to choose? Couldn't you take this job, pay your bills, and continue to figure out what you want in the long term?"

"OMG yes! Why didn't I think of that?!"

Answer: Anne didn't think of that because her default mode was to frame everything as a crisis. When you do that, you can't even see all of the good stuff right in front of you.

My personal struggles have been with approval-seeking and perfectionism, and let me tell you, perfectionism is a noose you knot yourself. For most of my life, perfectionism really got in the way of my happiness. Big time. I wouldn't say I've totally slayed that dragon, but I've made huge strides, and I'm much happier for it. If you struggle with some of this stuff and don't deal with it, it's going to affect your work, and even if you change careers you're just going to carry it with you to your next job.

So, the question is, *Is the problem your job, or is it you?*

Learning that *you* are the problem can be damn unpleasant. But it's also empowering. If the problem resides within you, then so does the solution.

Maybe you don't have the confidence to speak up at work. Maybe you're doing too much work with not enough pay and you're burning out. Well, did you ask for a raise? Did you ask for a reduced workload? You have to ask for the things you want.

I have a friend who is consistently disappointed with her husband for not doing his share of the work with the house and the kids. But she won't ask for help or tell him what she needs. In fact, she pretends everything is fine. Meanwhile, she carries all this accumulated resentment with her. Your spouse is not a mind reader. Neither is your boss. You may or may not get what you want, but you gotta ask.

What's one thing you can do this week to start dealing with one of your issues? Make it a baby step or a big step. Maybe it's reading a helpful book. Maybe it's speaking to a doctor or therapist. Maybe it's having a conversation that is long overdue, or talking about it with a friend or colleague. Maybe it's joining some kind of support group, or working with a coach, or enrolling in a workshop. Or maybe it's just a commitment to notice when the issue creeps up, so you can start to self-correct.

Bailing on your job without examining your issues is like bailing water out of a boat with a hole in the bottom. It won't work. You can bail until the point of exhaustion, but you're still going to get wet. That's what happens when you focus only on the symptoms of a problem instead of the cause.

Let me be clear. Just because you have some issues (and we *all* have issues) it's no reason to stay in a job that sucks until you've battled all of your demons and slayed all of your psychological dragons. That takes a lifetime — if you're lucky.

If you're yearning for a change in your career, do it. But deal with your baggage and personal issues, too. If not, they'll follow you to your next destination. Ask yourself, *How am I getting in my own way?* and work on that stuff alongside any other ambitions you have.

You are going to be a work in progress for your whole life. Don't let this stuff get in the way of making an important career change, but recognize that sometimes the internal changes we make are actually the ones that have the biggest impact.

Ask yourself,
*How am I getting
in my own way?*

SELFISH

The word *selfish* has a bad rap. I get it. Being "concerned chiefly or only with yourself" seems like kind of an asshole move. But is that always the case? I don't think so. The "Fuck you, suckers!" variety of selfishness deserves its critics, but what about the kind of selfishness that simply means you're putting yourself first?

I dove into this with a client the other day. She was reluctant to ask for some much-needed vacation time at work. She felt greedy, guilty, and selfish for taking time off when her colleagues would have to cover her workload while she was gone.

"You mean the way you did for them when *they* were on vacation?" I asked.

We talked about feeling bad for simply asking for what was rightfully hers, and the word *selfish* kept coming up. This word often comes up with many of my (mostly female) clients who have trouble asking for what they want. So I asked the question: What's so wrong with being selfish, anyway? What's wrong with putting yourself first?

What's wrong with asking for your vacation time? What's wrong with not being the last one to leave the office every night? What's wrong with not picking up the slack for your colleagues?

I'll feel bad.
I'll feel guilty.
I'll feel greedy.
It's selfish.

These are the typical responses.

What do you think is going to happen if you put yourself first?

It might seem selfish.

AND?

Somebody might not like it.

AND?

Somebody might not like me.

AHA.

The fear of being perceived as selfish is often about the fear of not being liked. So you work hard to make sure you don't ruffle any feathers or make waves. You're careful not to step on any toes, which *seems* really nice on the surface, but it's not altruistic at all — it's self-defense against disapproval.

Except that kind of passive self-defense doesn't work very well because you never get what you want. Everybody likes you because everybody gets their way. You're easy, accommodating — likable. So there you are, as likable as the month of May, with your finger perpetually stuck in the hole in the dam, gritting your teeth through your forced smile and waving at passersby.

I get wanting everybody to like you. I'm *verrrrry* familiar with that old tune. But how can we expect to get what we want (and deserve) unless we stand up and ask for it? . . . Unless we're a little selfish?

It's like we're always waiting for permission to finally get what we deserve — our recognition, our reward, our day in the sun. But the truth is, sometimes that day only comes because you grab it and make it happen. Because you claim it.

I can't believe I'm about to quote Dr. Phil, but he always said, "You teach people how to treat you." And you know what? That sweet, mustachioed, bumper sticker wisdom–spouting guy was right. You *do* teach people how to treat you, and if you don't put yourself first, who's going to?

It's time to take your finger out of the dam and put yourself first. Some people won't like it, but not everybody has to.

We like to think of approval-seeking and people-pleasing as primarily female behaviors, but it isn't so. Just ask any man who is shackled to his white horse.

If you don't put yourself first, who's going to?

Society continues to feed men archaic messages about what it means to be a man. *Real men provide. Work first, happiness second, or not at all. Real men are strong. Real men rescue.* In one of her TED talks, Dr. Brené Brown talks about an encounter with a man who said, "My wife and daughters would rather see me die up on my white horse than fall down." I'm certain he's not alone in feeling that way, given the constrained view of modern manhood. The popular image of modern man, reduced to worker, provider, rescuer, and rock, makes it difficult, if not almost impossible, for men to put themselves first. A man on a white horse is just as miserable as a woman with her finger in the dam.

As oppressive as these roles feel, nobody ends up on a white horse or with their finger in the dam without implicitly agreeing to do so. The solution, then, means walking away from the dam, getting off the horse, and coming out from behind the desk. It means giving yourself permission to put yourself first, to be a little selfish. If you don't, who will?

FEAR

IT'S NOT ABOUT SLAYING YOUR DRAGON.
IT'S ABOUT LEARNING TO RIDE IT.

CAREERHACK

Desperate for a career change, have you ever taken to Google to see what your safest options are? Or if not for yourself, perhaps for your son who just graduated from college, or your daughter who will apply for university next year? C'mon, fess up.

I work with a lot of people who have spent a great deal of energy forecasting sure bets when choosing their career. They come to me five, 10, 20 years later and say things like:

"My dad said people will always need accountants, so I just picked that."

"I love the security of my government job, but I feel like I'm dying inside."

"The research showed it was a stable career, and I

could make a ton of cash, but I don't actually like being a pharmacist."

These people *thought* they were doing their due diligence, but in each case, it led them down the wrong path.

If the research-it-to-death approach sounds like your own, I'd like to gently suggest that you may be looking for direction in the wrong places. Outsourcing decisions about your future in the name of security *seems* less risky than following your intuition, but it rarely leads to a good career fit.

I'm about to tell you a secret that, frankly, not a lot of people want to hear:

There is no safe choice. Or right choice. Or wrong choice. The world is, and will always be, filled with change and uncertainty — even when it comes to your career. Does that make you want to jump off a cliff? Give you hives? I know, I know . . . me too. But the truth is, there is no way to prepare enough to guarantee yourself a secure and risk-free career. And that really sucks.

Careers are rarely predictable. The predictable ones are the exception, not the rule, and the myth of playing it safe can box you in. Most people make a career change because they want more freedom. But the minute you start considering only the surest and safest bets, you paint yourself into a corner. You're back in the box.

Career security is like a mirage — you see it shimmering in the distance, but it's not really there. Just ask any union employee who finds himself out of work when his plant closes, or the woman who gives 30 years of her life slogging away for one company only to be unceremoniously dumped during a merger. You can always be fired, downsized, or replaced. Your company could fold. The economy could tank. Depressing, I know. Nobody wants to learn that their ironclad plan was really just a house of cards, but it happens all the time. There are no lifetime guarantees.

I'm not trying to be a downer. I don't want to make you throw up your hands and say, *Well, fuck the whole thing then. I'm off to live in the woods*. What I'm saying is that since there are no lifetime guarantees, you might as well make your career choices based on what you actually want to do instead of what you think (or what someone told you to think) is a safe bet — because there's no such thing.

Nobody wants to learn that their ironclad plan was really just a house of cards.

Be careful of whose career advice you take — including mine. If it doesn't feel right, it's not for you. Be careful, also, of what "expert data" you use to help you make your career decisions. Career quizzes, leadership assessments, and aptitude inventories are at best helpful tools for self-awareness, not the final authority on your future. Same goes for the stats and reports that forecast things like "the most stable careers for the next decade." Careful there. Those numbers change annually. Sometimes quarterly. Don't bet your future on that.

The truth is, you can't hack a happy career. Or a safe and secure one. Oddly enough, this is empowering. Knowing that there are no 100 percent guarantees frees you from the pressure to fall in line, follow the crowd, and suck it up, all for the sake of "security." It lets you off the hook for following someone else's advice. Sure, do your research. Talk things out with people you trust. But feel free to call bullshit the next time someone tells you that their solution is a sure thing.

FEAR
DISGUISED AS PRACTICALITY

Jim Carrey is a comedy genius, a maker of multi-million-dollar blockbuster movies, and a Golden Globe winner. But did you see the graduation speech he gave at the Maharishi University of Management? Wow. Now *that* was something.

He talked about his father, who desperately wanted to work in comedy but took the safe route and became an accountant instead, only to fail at that anyway. He told the young souls on the doorstep of their careers to choose love over fear because, unfortunately, "so many of us choose our path out of fear disguised as practicality."

Fear disguised as practicality. BOOM. From the lips of the guy who played Ace Ventura. The dude is wise.

Have you ever used scare tactics to force yourself

down a career path you don't really want to be on? You work hard to convince yourself that a certain path is really the only choice. It may not be what you want, but it's the *practical* thing to do. That's exactly what Jim Carrey was talking about — fear disguised as practicality.

Maybe you feel pressured to work in a certain field because you happen to have a degree in that area. Or because you heard that it was a safe bet. Or because you were encouraged to do so by someone you love and respect. None of those things are reasons enough to build a career in any field unless you also enjoy the work. If it doesn't float your boat, it isn't worth it.

Similarly, just because you happen to be good at something doesn't mean you have to make a career of it. If you don't enjoy something, don't spend your life doing it. It's not just about *skills*; it's also about *desire*.

Seems like a no brainer, right? Yet, there are gazillions of people out there slogging away at stuff they don't like because it *seems* like the practical thing to do, the obvious choice, the road most traveled — the path of least resistance.

Things I'm good at but choose not to make a career of include research, proposals, data collection, statistical reports . . . and the list goes on. I choose not to make a career of these things because I find them kind of, well, boring. They feel "meh" to me.

And you know what? Meh isn't good enough. Not for me. Not for you. Not for anybody.

Make a mental list of the things you're good at, but don't really like. The stuff that feels safe, but boring. Write it down if you want.

Got it? Good. Now . . .

Do not make a career of doing those things!

That's it.

You have enough interests and enough talents that you don't need to be grinding away at stuff that bores you to tears or cripples your soul. What you want to do is move from a *meh* to a *hell yes, bring it on!* Or at least to a *hey, this is cool*.

Why do people settle for *meh* in their careers when they could go for a big fat *YES*? Four words: *fear disguised as practicality*.

Giving in to fear disguised as practicality is the surest way to guarantee that you have a career identity crisis later in life, when you feel heavy regret for not going after what you wanted in the first place. And you don't want to be that guy.

Assuming you don't want to live a life filled with regret, your only option is to be honest with yourself, as frightening as that might seem. Are you rationalizing about what you think you *should* be doing just because you're afraid of what you really want? You wouldn't be the first.

Enough with the sad rationalizations. Admit what you want. Then work up the guts to go after it.

Meh isn't good enough.

IS ALL
FEAR BAD?

We often think of fear as a bad thing — for example, the fear that paralyzes us from taking action and going after what we want. But the truth is, you may also experience great anxiety and discomfort as you move toward some very wonderful (but still very scary) things. This begs the question: *Is all fear bad?*

The answer is no.

So how are you supposed to know if you should surrender to your fear or ride it out?

The best way to do this is to try to figure out what *type* of fear you are feeling. Is it fear + aversion or fear + anticipation?

One feels like oppression, and the other feels like opportunity. One feels like shackles, and the other feels like freedom. One feels like push, and the other feels like pull. One feels like submissive resignation, and the other feels like steeling yourself for an exciting challenge.

Remember tobogganing as a kid? You trudged to the top of the biggest hill, positioned your toboggan in juuuuust the right spot, took a deep breath, and pushed off, shrieking and giggling all the way down. That moment before you push off? *That's* fear + anticipation.

It's the same fear and anticipation you feel when you reach the tipping point on a roller coaster. Or the fear and anticipation you felt when you learned how to ride a bike. It's that *holy shit, I can't believe I'm actually doing this* feeling.

Fear and aversion, on the other hand, feels like brussels sprouts. Or like going on a date with someone you hate. Or kissing Jabba the Hutt. *Ick. Hell no.*

Think of a career option that you're not entirely sure if you should approach or avoid. Hold it in your mind.

Now, does it feel more like fear + anticipation or fear + aversion?

Here's my advice: Steer clear of the things that feel like fear + aversion (that icky brussels sprouts feeling), and move toward the things that feel like fear + anticipation (that *holy shit, I can't believe I'm actually doing this* feeling). It will still be scary, but the *right* kind of scary.

FEARLESS,
MY ASS

I have a client — a coach who is gearing up to start her practice — who expressed admiration for the ballsy vibe of my own business. She asked, "How did you become so *fearless*?!"

To which I replied, and I quote, "Are you fucking kidding me? I'm scared most of the time."

That was a big surprise to her, so I thought it was about time we aired this fear thing out.

My particular brand of fear usually involves worrying about what people will think of me. I worry way too much about how I may be perceived. I like to say that I'm a recovering approval-seeker, but it's a long road, baby.

We are all just scared humans, every one of us. Anyone who says they don't care about what people think is either flat-out lying or way more evolved than the other 99 percent of us (but I have a feeling it's usually the former, not the latter).

When people talk about being fearless, I think what they're actually talking about is being *brave*, but the words *fearless* and *brave* are not interchangeable. Nor are the words *fear* and *bravery* opposites. Fear isn't the opposite of bravery, it's a prerequisite. You can't have bravery without fear. Fear comes first.

How are you supposed to know if you should surrender to your fear or ride it out?

And that means fear is an opportunity to show yourself what you're really made of.

So let's just go ahead and admit that life is one big scary adventure — wonderful and surprising and exciting, yes, but white-knuckling it is also part of the deal.

At the risk of sounding neurotic (See? I'm even afraid of what I'm about to say), here are some of the fearful thoughts that ran through my head today:

Ugh. Typo. People are going to think I'm an idiot.

I hope that Facebook post didn't offend anybody.
Maybe I should edit it. Or remove it.

So-and-so is acting strange. Is she mad at me?
Why would she be mad at me?

Maybe I shouldn't have told people about that goal of
mine. If I don't achieve it, I'll be so embarrassed.

I hope that thing I said didn't sound too braggy.
I don't want people to think I'm arrogant.

I hope that thing I said didn't sound too apologetic.
I don't want people to think I'm a wuss.

What if that thing I wrote isn't my idea at all?
What if I read it in passing somewhere,
and I stole it without even knowing it?

What if that mistake I made comes
back to bite me in the ass?

Someday someone is going to figure out that
I'm just winging it, and then the whole damn
house of cards will come crashing down.

And the list goes on.

With fearful thoughts on parade, what's a person to do?

We assume we have to conquer our fear, battle our demons, and slay our dragons before we can move forward, but it's not true. It's not about slaying your dragon. It's about learning to ride it.

The part of the brain that regulates fear, the amygdala, is often called the *lizard brain*. That's because it's the most primitive part of the brain, the part we have in common with our prehistoric ancestors. It's why I like to think of fear as a jittery little lizard, easily spooked and quick to flee from mortal danger — danger like, say, the sweet little butterfly floating across its path.

The lizard brain is *always* on high alert, ready to flee the scene or fight to the death. When your fear is at its absolute worst, it feels less like a skittish little lizard and more like a raging, fire-breathing dragon — and there's no way you're going to win that battle, right? You're simply no match for it. That's why you don't *slay* the dragon. You can't. Instead, you *befriend* the dragon, and you *ride* it.

Befriending the dragon means getting really curious and really quiet. It means approaching your fear with wonder and intrigue, and spending some time with it. Slowly, gently, you approach your fear, and eventually you see the dragon for what it is — a frightened beast. Not an enemy to defeat, but a companion for the journey.

AMBITION

JUST BECAUSE YOU *CAN* DO
SOMETHING DOESN'T MEAN YOU *SHOULD*,
UNLESS YOU ALSO *WANT* TO.

DON'T
FIGHT YOUR CURVES

I'm a curvy girl. I carry a little extra junk in the trunk, and also some in the middle.

I can't say it's something I'm super psyched about. Sometimes I wish my lovely lady lumps were a little more lovely and a little less . . . ample. I'd like to say I don't fight my curves, but sometimes I do. That's just the truth.

I'm also a curvy girl metaphorically. I'll think I'm going to go straight in one direction, but then I end up curving off the path somehow — making a loop, U-turn, or bend somewhere along the way. Always a slight change of plans.

Very little in my career has been a straight shot. Here's what I mean:

My undergraduate degree is in journalism, but I didn't start writing until more than a decade after that. I was doing other stuff.

My fascination with workplace psychology took a huge U-turn, from focusing on theory (conducting research) to practice (becoming a career coach).

I'm a teacher at heart. I used to teach from boring university textbooks. Now I develop my own (way more fun) online courses.

I love helping people in transition. I used to help students transition to the next phase of their formal education. Now I help them start their careers.

The essence of what I'm after rarely changes. But getting there? The path is never quite what I imagined it would be, never a straight line. There are always loops, twists, and turns. It's curvy.

Since I'm a Type A, go-getter kind of gal, this used to frustrate the hell out of me (and occasionally it still does). Wouldn't a straight line from A to B be better? More efficient?

More efficient, yes.

Better, no.

This way of navigating your career — the curvy way — takes longer, and it rarely looks the way you think it will. It's also *way* better. It means you get to do things in a way that is uniquely you. Everything is a perfect fit when you do it that way. Yet occasionally I've had to remind myself, *Girl, don't fight your curves. They're working for you.*

My curves are working for me every time I give myself permission to go off course and quit something I hate . . . only to end up finding something even better.

My curves are working for me every time I experiment with something new . . . and end up loving it.

My curves are working for me every time I'm scared to take the road less traveled, but do it anyway . . . and it totally pays off.

It *is* scary to go off course, take a turn, head for an exit, circle around. But you know what's scarier? Heading dead straight toward the wrong thing. That's a collision just waiting to happen every time.

Maybe you forced yourself to go to business school to study finance when you really wanted to study psychology . . . and now you hate working in finance.

Maybe you won't leave the big city you hate for a simpler life in a small community you love . . . and you resent it every single day.

Maybe you really want to make something of your own, but you refuse to get off the corporate ladder . . . even though the climb is crippling your soul.

Maybe you hate being an entrepreneur, but your pride prevents you from dissolving your business and taking a job . . . even though you'd be infinitely happier if you did.

Maybe 10, 15, 20 years of success in one field is preventing you from making a career change you really want to make ... even though you're bored to tears with your work.

If the career path you're on doesn't fit, it just doesn't fit. End of story. Forcing it won't make it fit better.

Ever tried to wrestle your way into a pair of jeans that are too small? It sucks. Sure, you might get those suckers on, but you're going to walk around feeling a little cranky and agitated (and probably with plumber butt). You can't breathe. Everything pinches. It's like that with a career that doesn't fit, too.

Don't fight your curves. Try something else on. Something that's a better fit.

If the career path you're on doesn't fit, it just doesn't fit. End of story. Forcing it won't make it fit better.

$UCCE$$

How successful are you? Take a minute to think about it.

Now, what criteria did you use to evaluate your success? If you're like most people, you probably considered your income, job title, degrees, accolades, and material things like your home, car, or maybe even your collection of designer shoes, bags, or watches. Maybe you considered your physical health or your marital status.

If I'm being honest, these are some of the things that cross my mind, too.

Do I consider myself successful? I do. I created a pretty awesome business, I'm well respected in my field, and I have a bunch of degrees. I write for some high-profile publications. My home is lovely. My relationships are strong.

On the other hand, I don't own my home. I sold my condo when I divorced. I'm also overweight. Oh, and I quit my Ph.D. 93 pages into my dissertation. From the outside, that may not look like a smashing success.

But what do we mean by "success" anyway?

A friend of mine says the word *success* is like the word *god*. If you ask 100 people what it means, every one of them will have a different answer. He's right.

On one level, we understand that *real* success is about happiness. We know this. And yet . . .

And yet most of us (even those of us — ahem — who help people get happy for a living) easily confuse success for happiness. At least until we wise up.

Look up the word *success* and you'll find a definition like "the attainment of wealth, position, honors, or the like," and synonyms like "accomplishment," "prosperity," and "fame." I have nothing against the word *success* or even its traditional definition. It's just a word, after all. But let's call it what it is. It's an external benchmark for performance and attainment — a measuring stick.

Measuring sticks have their place, especially in the work world. But if you're looking for personal fulfillment, it's not likely that traditional measures of success are going to get you there.

As a society, we have come to believe that success — stuff and status — is the yellow brick road. Follow it and we'll most certainly arrive at the Emerald City of happiness. There's nothing inherently wrong with wanting stuff, status, wealth, or acclaim, but it's a mistake to assume that they pave the way to happiness and fulfillment. And therein usually lies the problem. We strive for success, but it's actually happiness and fulfillment we're after.

The word *success* has been thrown around so frequently, and in such varied contexts, that we have forgotten what it really means. It is vague, all-encompassing, a catch-all.

Success dangles the things we *think* will make us happy (stuff and status). It's a lure, shiny and seductive, but here's the hook — you can do everything right in the pursuit of traditional success, but happiness and personal fulfillment are not guaranteed. In other words, success isn't enough. And the thing is, we don't actually want the stuff and status. What we want is the way we *think* the stuff and status is going to make us feel.

A popular formula for success and happiness that is guaranteed to fail is the following: *When I have* (insert measure of success here) *I will be happy.* Success and happiness are two different things, and one doesn't necessarily lead to the other. Don't get them confused.

> We strive for success,
> but it's actually happiness
> and fulfillment we're after.

EASY THERE, TIGER

I am what one might affectionately call a "keener" — or, on a bad day, a "frazzled and perfectionistic over-achiever." I'm working on it. This is pervasive in all areas of my life, personal and professional, but high up in the Rocky Mountains, away from my day-to-day work, I was reminded of the value of pacing myself.

I was on a hiking trip, the first half with a women's outdoor adventure travel company and the second half hiking on my own. The group hikes were a tough slog, both physically and mentally, as I struggled to keep up. Fueled by fear of impending humiliation, I huffed and puffed alongside a group of women who were both older and in better shape than me.

During my solo hikes, however, something different happened. I hit my stride. I was able to hike farther on my own than I could in a group. Significantly farther. Suddenly, I was able to hike *double* the distance I had done with the group. I would chalk it up to conditioning, but the change happened literally overnight. I'm convinced that the difference was that I was going at my own pace. I wasn't wearing myself out in a frantic scramble to keep up.

At work and in life, I have always done better when I do things at my own pace. Not that this comes naturally to me. *Au contraire*. Like so many others, I whip myself into a frenzy when playing the comparison game. Tracking myself against the progress of others — their careers, their achievements, their milestones — usually does nothing but slow me down, as panic inevitably sets in when I realize I'm not at the very front of the pack.

Perhaps you know a little something about this, too?

Have you ever found yourself on a path you had no interest in being on, just for the sake of keeping up with the Joneses? One day you look up, take a good look around you, and realize you're on the brink of burnout (or bored to tears) — all for a career trajectory you don't even want.

When you're frantically trying to keep up or get ahead of the pack, sometimes you forget to check in and see if the pack is actually headed in the right direction. Ever gone for a promotion just for the sake of it? Purchased a bigger house, better car, or more stuff because that was just what everyone else was doing? If so, repeat after me: *Easy there, Tiger.*

Sometimes we get so caught up in getting ahead that we forget ourselves in the scramble. I'm a firm believer in the pursuit of growth and development, so I believe it's important to push yourself. The whole idea of *pacing* yourself is, admittedly, a newer concept to me, and I'm finding it so very important.

Sometimes we get so caught up in getting ahead that we forget ourselves in the scramble.

Are your people — your company, your colleagues, your industry — headed in the right direction? By the right direction, I mean a direction *you* want to be heading in. There's no sense in trying to keep up if they're not going where you want to go. In fact, you may find that your colleagues are leading you astray, farther from the place you actually want to be.

If the people you work and associate with aren't really *your* people at all, you need to reassess. Maybe you're at the wrong organization, or even in the wrong field, building networks with people you have no interest in associating with. If so, it's time to take a deep breath and make a change.

If the people around you *are* your people (You love your industry! You love your colleagues! You love your work!), you're headed in the right direction. Getting to this point is half the battle. But even when you're in the right field of work, it's tempting to compare yourself to others. Resist the urge to track your progress against everyone else's. Take stock of what you want, how you want to get there, and at what pace. Remind yourself that *your* pace is the best pace for you. This is harder than you'd think.

You'll feel pressured to keep up with the keeners or to stop and help those lagging behind. Remember that you don't have to speed up or slow down for anyone else. You don't need to feel inadequate for not keeping up. You also don't have to feel guilty for leaving others in your dust. Your pace is your business. Their pace is theirs. Leave it at that.

ENOUGH
IS ENOUGH

As the notorious 20th-century poet Christopher Wallace said, "Mo money, mo problems."

Actually, mo money often isn't the problem; it's what you give up to get it.

Grasping after more — more money, more success, more (insert your personal brand of carrot here) — can leave you gasping for air like a hamster on a wheel.

Society tells us what we should want, and that we should want as much of it as possible. But sometimes getting more money and more success don't feel as good as we thought it would. So we start chasing the next thing, and then the next thing after that. It's a vicious cycle (not to mention exhausting).

So I've been thinking about the word "enough" a lot lately — both for myself and for my clients.

Last week I had to turn away some prospective clients. Wait, let me rephrase that: last week I *chose* to turn away some prospective clients, either because our schedules conflicted or because the fit just wasn't right.

I *could* have rearranged my schedule and taken them on, but I chose not to.

Why? Because I have enough. More isn't better.

I've been in business for just a few years, so I'm not exactly making it rain (yet). But I have enough. And enough is, surprisingly, enough. Who knew?

For most of my life, I've had a voracious appetite for success. *More, more, more* was my personal motto. Things have changed.

Don't get me wrong. Ambition is a wonderful thing. But gluttonous grasping isn't. So I've mellowed out a little. I'm ambitious, not insatiable. *Big* difference.

Recently a new client asked me how many appointments I take each day. Ideally, it's four. Five max.

"That's it?" he asked.

Yup. Logistically speaking, I could see six clients a day. I could also take evening and weekend appointments. But I don't. More isn't better.

Similarly, a few colleagues have told me, *You could save so much time and get even more clients if you had an automated scheduling system!*

True. But I have enough. More isn't better.

I work from home on Fridays. It feels like such a treat. I don't set an alarm, so I wake up when my body wants to. I schlep around in jogging pants and spend the day writing or working on administrative stuff. I take a long lunch, and I enjoy a manicure, a hot bath, or a sunny stroll. I love that I can do that.

But if I took clients on Fridays, I could make more money! Isn't that worth giving up a few simple pleasures?

Hell no. More isn't better.

If I was burning out or taking on more than I wanted to, I'd be a pretty shitty coach — not to mention a bad example. I run a business that helps people get happier at work, so you bet your ass I'm walking the talk. With any choice, you gain something, and you give something up. That's how it works. It just depends on what you want and what you're willing to give up. The scales will tip differently for different people.

I recently helped a woman decide if she wanted to have a third child. She struggled with the decision because there would be less disposable income. Her friends had bigger houses than she did, and more money. A third child would mean keeping the smallish house, less clothes shopping, and fewer vacations per year. But after crunching the numbers, that was it. Financially, these were the only drawbacks. She and her husband both wanted a baby, and they could easily handle all of the other expenses. They had enough clothes. Enough vacations. A big enough house.

Once you have enough, more isn't necessarily better.

Now, if you *don't* have enough, that's a different story. Not having enough sucks.

I kept my teaching gig for a year before I took my business full-time because I wouldn't have had enough without it. And I sure as hell took the occasional Friday appointment when I was first starting my business. Once I took a Saturday appointment, but it didn't feel right. I like to rest and recharge on the weekends, so I never booked another Saturday. Ask yourself: What are you willing to give up in order to gain something else?

Once you pass the threshold of enough, it's time to re-evaluate. Once you have enough, the whole game changes. So it's worth asking yourself, *How much is enough?* Really think about it. Maybe you reached enough a long time ago.

> With any choice,
> you gain something, and
> you give something up.

ENLIGHTENED
AMBITION

When I want something, I go after it with laser focus, and I work hard enough that I usually get it. So, over the years I've developed a sense that I can achieve pretty much whatever goal I put my mind to. That should be a good thing, right?

Well, sometimes.

That kind of focused drive works wonders when your goals are closely aligned with what you actually want. Work feels like play. Energy abounds. Ideas flow freely.

However, that kind of striving is draining if your goals aren't in alignment with what you really want. The pursuit feels forced. Each step is labored and heavy. It's exhausting. I bet you know what this feels like. I'm guessing so because many of us set goals that are really out of whack with our true desires.

Sometimes we blindly strive for things we *think* we want, or things we think we *should* want, which may or may not be what we *actually do* want.

Crazy, I know. But it's easier than you'd think to confuse those things.

Sometimes we blindly strive for things we *think* we want, or things we think we *should* want, which may or may not be what we *actually do* want.

When I help people set goals for their careers, one of the most important questions I can ask them is "why?" *Why* are they setting that particular goal? Why is a simple question (I mean, we've been asking it since we were toddlers!), but it helps us determine if a goal is aligned with what we *actually* want.

A while back, I noticed that some of my own goals felt heavy, oppressive. It was time to start asking myself why I wanted what I wanted. Once I started asking myself why,

I learned that some of the goals I had set had little to do with my actual desires.

I like to think I'm someone who generally has her shit together (okay, nobody has all of their shit together . . . not all at once, anyway), but I was going about some of my own goal setting in the wrong way. This struck me as especially ironic because I get paid to help other people set and achieve their goals. Alas, as the saying goes, we teach what we need to learn.

For example, right beside my refrigerator, in black Sharpie marker, I had scribbled the goal "Own a beautiful lakefront cottage." Surely that goal couldn't be misdirected, right? I'm a nature lover. And besides, doesn't everyone want that? To my surprise, it turns out I do not.

I asked myself why I wanted a beautiful lakefront cottage in the same way I ask my clients why they set a particular career goal.

I want to own a beautiful lakefront cottage.

WHY?

Because I feel most like myself in nature.
Because I think clearly and feel connected in nature.

Oh. I see that I want to *be in nature*, not necessarily to *own property*. Hell, that's easy. I live in a city with lots

Ambition is great,
but only when
it's aligned
with what you
really want.

of beautiful trails. My parents own a farm. I live within walking distance of some gorgeous parks. It might take me a decade to save up for a lakefront cottage, but I can go for a hike this afternoon.

Funnily enough, right this second I'm writing this chapter from a little off-grid cabin in the woods. I rented it for a whole week. I'm sitting on a big orange Muskoka chair wearing jogging pants and flip-flops while I listen to the wind shuffle the maple leaves. I feel grounded and steady and wise. I feel small and expansive all at once. Yes, *that* is what I want. And I can certainly make room for more of that in my life. Problem solved.

I went through this same process of inquiry with each of my goals. Eighty percent of them were already right on track, but tweaking or ditching the other 20 percent felt downright liberating! Setting goals that are aligned with your true desires (and ditching the ones that aren't) is what I call *enlightened ambition*.

Here's how you do it:

1. State your goal.
2. Drill down to the "why."
3. Tweak or toss anything not aligned with what you *really* want.

That's it. It seems almost too simple to work, but sometimes simple is best. Enlightened ambition is a stripped-down kind of goal setting, and it's as much about tossing what's not working as it is about pursuing what is.

I don't really want to do this MBA. It making me sick. I'd love to take a photography class instead.

My boss looks miserable. I don't want to end up like her. Why am I even bothering to apply for this promotion?

Maybe I should forget about going for partner at the firm. I rarely see my kids as it is.

I don't want to keep pouring money into a failing business. A steady job would feel so much better.

If you're chasing after something because you're looking for approval or status, or because it's what's expected of you, it's just not worth it. You'll get to the finish line and think, *This is it? THIS is what I killed myself for?* Talk about a letdown.

We're a goal-obsessed society. Stronger, better, faster. More, more, more. Striving and driving and pushing and climbing. There's nothing wrong with ambition. Ambition is great, but only when it's aligned with what you really want.

Sometimes the best thing to do is let go of some old goals that simply aren't serving you anymore. Lighten your load. Let 'em go. Make room. It's time your goals started working for you again, and not the other way around.

THE
SEDUCTION OF SHOULD

Let's talk about the word *should*, shall we?

It's a word I hear often from the people I work with, especially when they're resisting what they want to do in favor of something else, all in the name of doing what's most logical or dutiful or socially acceptable.

I should really get around to organizing my files.

I should really get to the gym more this year.

I should stay a few extra hours
at work tonight since everyone else is.

I should probably forget about
building my own business. Too risky.

I should probably just keep the job I have.
At least the benefits are good.

Ever notice how nobody ever says the word *should* with passion or enthusiasm? It's always a little bit deflated, a little bit defeated, uttered with tired resignation. Not exactly inspiring, is it?

Should isn't very inspiring, but it can be seductive. It charms you with stories of duty and propriety and whispers promises of safety, security, acceptance, immunity, and refuge. But *should* is an ironhanded master. It raises its fist whenever you try to loosen its grip.

Should is something to endure, to put up with — to suffer through, sustain, and tolerate. Or else. *Should* is quick to remind you where your place is and what might happen if you step out of line. Stray too far from *should* and you'll find yourself an utter failure, a laughingstock, a pariah — disgraced and exiled from everything and everyone you love.

Ever notice how nobody ever says the word *should* with passion or enthusiasm?

Art school? You should really
go to law school instead.

Travel? You should save that for retirement.

Work as a massage therapist?
You should support the family business.

Freelance work? You should
hang on to that union job of yours.

I'm no stranger to *should* myself. In fact, I've danced very intimately with *should* for most of my life. *Should* likes to remind me about what other people will think. What other people think (or, more accurately, what I think they *might* think) has often kept me from doing what I want in favor of doing what I thought I was supposed to want (things like grinding through my old career path in academia). I wobbled under the heaviness of these things. I was like Atlas trying to hold up the world, but the psychological weight brought me to my knees. I felt like a failure, crushed by my inability to bear the weight of the things I thought I should do.

I now have a much cooler, arms-length relationship with *should*. I know it has strung me along and led me astray in the past. I remember what the snare and the shackles felt like, and I'm keeping my distance. I hope you will too.

AMBITION
AMNESIA

Ever feel like you keep making the same mistakes over and over?

You keep dating the same kind of person, and it never works out. You make a budget, but you always overspend anyway. You wait until the very last minute to get a project done even though you swore never to procrastinate like this again.

What's going on here? Why do we keep making the same mistakes over and over when our experience tells us we ought to know better by now? And why do mistakes like this keep showing up not only in our personal lives, but also in our careers?

You keep applying for jobs you know you'll never get — or worse, ones you know you'll hate. Or you keep overpromising and underdelivering at work. Or you keep giving 150 percent at the office even though you never get the credit you deserve. Or you bite off more than you can chew and end up burning out every time. Or you set goals that never actually make you feel good once you achieve them.

This is something I know a thing or two about. I work with a lot of people who have chased after the same kind of thing over and over, even though it doesn't make them happy. Hell, I have struggled with this myself. I call this *ambition amnesia* — selective memory when it comes to misguided pursuits of the past. We forget that a certain kind of goal never quite does it for us. We think it will be different *this* time, but instead of fireworks, it always ends with a lackluster fizzle. It's one big sad trombone looped and playing on repeat.

Ambition amnesia takes different forms for different people. Maybe you've experienced it yourself. See if you can find yourself in one of these groups:

COPYCATS

Don't know what kind of pursuits the Copycats have planned? Neither do they. They take their cues from friends and colleagues and simply follow along.

Did you hear that So-and-so applied for that promotion? I think it looks kind of boring, not to mention underpaid, but maybe I'll apply too.

> *So-and-so started her own consulting business. Hell, I could do that with my eyes closed. Yes, that's exactly what I should be doing!*

OMG, So-and-so is getting a master's degree! Do I need a master's degree?! I'm totally going to apply for a master's degree.

"I'll have what she's having" is the Copycat motto. Copycats are afraid of being left out or forgotten, so they just do what everyone else is doing, which actually makes them kind of, well, forgettable. Not to mention unfulfilled.

Copycats would be wise to keep their eyes on their own test paper. They may be surprised to learn they already have the answers.

GOLD STAR JUNKIES

Gold Star Junkies want approval, prestige, and status. They look *reeeeeally* good on paper. They seem to have all of their shit together — impressive resumes, many awards, accolades and accomplishments, and they're often light years ahead of their peers — but something is missing.

Notice the difference between push and pull.

They're so busy chasing the next gold star that they pause only briefly to enjoy their accomplishments. During what should be an incredible high, they're already thinking about their next fix, strung out on the need for more status and standing.

A lot of my clients are Gold Star Junkies. After landing on a career choice that she knew would make her happy, one of my clients said, "But what will people think? I'm capable of so much more!" If that sounds like you, I'll repeat what I said to her: "Yes, you are. You are capable of many things. The question is, what do you want? Just because you *can* do something doesn't mean you *should* do it — unless you also *want* to."

Constantly seeking approval is needy, stressful, and just plain exhausting. As a recovering Gold Star Junkie, I understand the lure of prestige and status all too well, but I've learned there's a big difference between striving for something to prove yourself or impress others and working toward something that actually lights you up.

If the pursuit feels forced, don't do it. If it feels like love, go for it. Notice the difference between push and pull.

HUNGRY GHOSTS

In Chinese Buddhist folklore, there are spirits called "hungry ghosts." As punishment for being greedy in life, these souls are given bloated, empty stomachs and minuscule mouths, too small for food to pass through. Hungry ghosts are doomed to roam the afterlife seeking to satisfy their voracious appetites, but nothing ever fills the void.

Some people are like that, too. A voracious, insatiable appetite keeps them grasping after more, more, more — more wealth, more stuff, more status — but more is never enough.

Hungry Ghosts have a lot in common with Gold Star Junkies, with one key difference. While Gold Star Junkies briefly pause to enjoy the fruits of their labor, Hungry Ghosts are never satisfied.

If your ambition is insatiable, and success never quite fills you up, maybe more isn't what you need.

BOY SCOUTS AND GIRL SCOUTS

Safety is number one for Scouts. They take their motto, "Always be prepared," very seriously. In fact, they're so busy being prepared that they forget to get a life. They don't get out much, and their pantry is always fully stocked in the event of the zombie apocalypse.

Boy Scouts and Girl Scouts are rigid rule followers who spend a lot of time justifying their safe and logical career choices (mostly to themselves). Time and time

Maybe more isn't what you need.

again, they're willing to settle for the safest, surest thing, but the problem is just that — it always feels like settling.

Boy and Girl Scouts might be happier in their careers if they remembered to loosen their neck scarves and live a little.

GOOD SOLDIERS

If you finally found the guts to quit your job and do what you love, but then your dad talked you into doing something else, there's a very good chance you're a Good Soldier.

Good Soldiers fall in line and do what they're expected to do. They take orders well, especially from authority figures like Mom, Dad, teachers, and mentors.

Actions that may look like cowardice from the outside are actually motivated by a sense of duty or a debt of gratitude. Good Soldiers don't want to let anyone down. They listen to people they respect and admire, but in the end it never makes them happy.

Good Soldiers might be more fulfilled in their careers if they stopped gritting their teeth and taking orders.

Are some of your own goals and habits getting in your way, time after time? If so, you have ambition amnesia. Next time you set yourself a certain type of career goal, ask yourself if you've been there before and if it actually made you happy. If not, it's time to reconsider the things you're chasing.

EVEN
BETTER

A few years ago, on one of my last days of summer vacation, I set out to do a 15-mile hike. I was trying to hike a
certain distance by the end of my vacation. I approached
the trailhead with a heavy pack and a hopeful heart. Ten
minutes into my hike, something wonderful happened — I
came across a family of Rocky Mountain bighorn sheep,
about seven or eight of them. Literally right in my path.

They weren't startled by my arrival, and they went
about their business munching greens amid the rocks. I had
a choice to make: I could snap a quick photo and be on my
way (I had a tight schedule and I wanted to make it back by
dark), or I could hang out with wild bighorn sheep. It was
a no-brainer. Sheep. Sheep all the way.

This meant I probably wouldn't achieve my hiking distance goal. But I took off my hiking pack and found a nice flat rock to sit on and enjoy the company of these quirky, curious creatures. Those sheep and I hung out for two hours.

I don't often give myself permission to change my mind. A set goal often sticks rigidly in the foreground, blocking all other (potentially better) options. But sometimes an even better opportunity lands in your lap, and you have to decide which road to take. It's actually a really awesome problem to have — to choose between something good and something even better.

If you've ever had a plan but unexpectedly found yourself in a toss-up situation, these words are for you: It's okay to change your mind. This doesn't come naturally for ambitious and rigid goal setters (like myself). Sometimes we get tunnel vision in our ambitious pursuits, and fail to consider the changing landscape around us.

Sticking to your guns is a good thing. But reframing and redefining a goal can also be good, especially if a better opportunity presents itself or if what you want changes. People evolve over time, and it's natural that your goals will evolve over time, too. We often forget this. Even when you find your "thing," you'll continue to change and grow. And you may find that 10 years down the road, your thing isn't really your thing anymore. Changing your mind isn't a failure. You just don't want what you used to want. Stubbornly sticking to an old path is foolish if it's no longer the path you want to be on.

Consider some of the big picture choices that people make: Do I pursue a graduate degree now or use this time to have children? Do I keep the steady job or move across the country to pursue something else? Make a career change or keep growing in my current career? Take the promotion or move to another company? Keep my corporate gig or start my own business? Which choice is the better option depends entirely on the person.

Changing your mind isn't a failure.

Of course, stakes like these are higher than choosing between a hike and some sheep. I've had to make some tough choices, too. I once chose to leave a solid, well-paying job in which I was well respected and worked with people I genuinely liked. But I felt pulled toward something else. I would be totally out of my element and make less money (way less, actually) on this new path. I knew this going in, and yet I chose to pursue it anyway. Was it a gamble? Absolutely. Do I regret it? Nope.

Each time you muster the guts to choose something you feel drawn toward — even if that thing wasn't a part of the original plan — you will be rewarded with more joy in your life. Don't get me wrong: The joy is often preceded by absolute terror and uncertainty, but it's worth the temporary discomfort. Plus, when you choose the path that feels right, you're never haunted by the question "what if?" Nobody wants to look back 10, 20, 30 years from now with regret.

I know what you're thinking. *But don't you still have to have a plan for big choices about your career? Isn't it irresponsible just to throw caution to the wind?* Yes and no. You should absolutely listen to your gut, but the gut and the brain need to work as a team. A major choice like making a career change requires first figuring out what you want (gut), and then figuring out how to make it happen (brain). If you go purely on gut, you may find yourself up and quitting your job with no plan to pay the bills. If you go purely on brain, you're likely to reason yourself into sticking with the surest, safest thing, despite your desires.

Whether it's a choice about what you do with your day or what you do with your career, every choice you make determines the course of your life. Choose wisely.

MONEY

YOU ARE NOT GOING TO LIVE
IN A VAN DOWN BY THE RIVER.

THE CHEESEMAKER
AND THE IPHONE

I'd like to tell you the story of the cheesemaker and the iPhone.

A client of mine, Jennifer, worked as an investment banker for a big, powerful firm you've probably heard of. She was good at her job, but she didn't enjoy it. She longed to do something totally different, to work as some kind of artisan or healer. She couldn't put her finger on what, exactly, she wanted to do (because she never allowed herself to think seriously about it), but it definitely wasn't investment banking.

Jennifer was especially intrigued by the thought of becoming an artisanal cheesemaker. It was honest work, and creative, and exacting, and it had this hearty, whole-some quality — things she longed for.

"That's not something I could ever do," she said. "I don't want to be poor. I like my iPhone."

We used this as a starting point to test some of her assumptions about money.

"Is it true that cheesemakers don't have iPhones?" I asked.

"I don't know. No. Oh my god, I'm being ridiculous."

We dug a little deeper and discovered one of Jennifer's beliefs about work and money: *People who pursue their passions can't make money doing so.*

Jennifer liked to think in black and white. In her mind, you could either do a job you hate and make a ton of cash, or do a job you love and be dirt poor. No iPhone. It was one or the other.

Without knowing it, Jennifer had tied the concepts of fulfilling work and poverty together. The truth is, in any profession you'll find a whole range of people — some who make a little money and some who make a lot.

I think about the cheesemaker and the iPhone when I work with people who have money fears — which is pretty

"Is it true that cheesemakers don't have iPhones?"

much everyone. Most people fear that they won't have enough money. Some people are afraid of having too much money. They resist it.

Maybe, like Jennifer, you have some assumptions about money and enjoyable work. Something like:

I'll never make money doing something I love.

OR

The only way to make money is
to suck it up and stick it out.

Perhaps you've tied together the concepts of money and greed:

People who make money are greedy, evil,
(insert your derogatory judgment here).

OR

I can't make a lot of money
and still be a good person.

Maybe you have some assumptions about people with money:

People with money are assholes.
I don't want to be like that.

OR

People with money are just lucky.

Related to these are assumptions about money and worthiness:

I'm not worthy of money.

OR

Other people get to make money. Not me.

Maybe you link money and happiness together:

I'll be happier when I have a lot of money.

OR

I have to make a lot of money now
so I can be happy later.

Many people have assumptions about money and time:

When I have a lot of money,
I'll have more free time.

OR (A RELATED ONE)

To make a lot of money,
you have to give up all of your time.

The list goes on and on and on.

Think about your own assumptions about money. How are they getting in your way? Maybe it's time to rewrite some of those stories.

A VAN
DOWN BY THE RIVER

Why is it that when we imagine going after the career we desire most, we conjure up an image of the worst possible outcome? We imagine a bleak future in which the pursuit of a dream ends in utter failure, and we end up hopeless and penniless, living in a van down by the river (just like *SNL*'s motivational speaker Matt Foley). Or under a bridge somewhere. Or wandering the streets like a vagabond.

Martha Beck likes to call these imagined scenarios "bag lady fears." They go something like this:

> *I can't possibly think about quitting my job to pursue*
> *something else because that pursuit will inevitably fail,*
> *and I'll lose all of my money, AND my house, AND*

my car, and I'll be forced to live out of a shopping cart
on the street corner, where all of the people I know will
point and laugh at me on their way to work.

Sound familiar?

Almost anyone who has ever considered a career change has imagined a ridiculous scenario something like this.

Maybe you picture your partner leaving you because you don't bring home the bacon anymore. Maybe it's your kids having to wear shabby clothes to school because you can't afford nice ones. Maybe it's your future self as a penniless old person living off food stamps. Or maybe it really is losing your house and moving into a van down by the river.

Think about your own bag lady story — the most extreme dystopian future you've ever imagined for yourself.

Now, imagine having a conversation with your best friend. She is miserable in her work and wants to make a change. Would you tell her that her future will end up just like the worst-case scenario story you've told yourself? I didn't think so. Why? Because that's not going to happen.

Pull yourself together, man.

You are an intelligent and talented person. You are not going to up and quit your job tomorrow without putting some kind of plan in place. Yes, there is some risk involved, but you're a smart cookie, and you would never let it come to that. Stop the horror stories already.

Plus, contrary to popular belief, having more money

does not make a person worry about money less. Even the super rich worry about money. There's a documentary called *The Queen of Versailles* about a stinking rich billionaire couple that does nothing but build hundred-million-dollar mansions and worry about money. You want to hate them for being shallow and clueless, but you can't because they're so damn human. They live in fear, and they don't know how to fix it.

So clearly the solution to worrying about money is not getting more money. Huh. Who knew? Sometimes the more money you have or make, the more you worry about losing it. It has more control over you. It's the "golden handcuffs" syndrome — when money feels more like shackles than freedom.

Stop the horror stories already.

A friend of mine, Jason, has a steady job working for the government. Great pay. Even better pension. He's miserable in his job, but he's afraid he'll lose too much if he leaves. He has golden handcuffs syndrome, so he's sticking it out. Jason is only in his 30s and not even at the halfway point in his career. It's going to be a long and unhappy road to that pension. It's sad because there are so many ways to make great money and build security. He just can't see past his fear, and so he's resigned himself to a miserable life until retirement day.

I get it. We all have money fears. And thinking about a career change stirs up those fears like nothing else. But money fears can paralyze you, keeping you from going after what you want. In other words, sometimes money fears can get in the way of your happiness.

Are your own money fears preventing you from living the life you want? Don't let irrational doomsday scenarios stop you from pursuing the happiness you deserve.

THE SHITTY END
OF THE STICK

How much money do you need?

This is not a rhetorical question. Nor is it laden with judgment. I'm not going to try to convince you that money doesn't matter and that you should just do what you love, financial worries be damned. Money *does* matter. It's what pays for the roof over your head and the food you eat.

But how much do you need, really? Be honest.

I asked myself this question when I left academia to build my own business. I was nearing the end of my Ph.D. and on track to become a professor. Full-time professors at business schools make six figures, easy. Between $150,000 and $200,000 in many cases. I certainly wasn't going to make that much in the first couple of years of my business, but I was okay with that. Hell, I was cool with making a quarter of that at the beginning.

Everyone answers the "How much money do you really need?" question a little differently.

Don't confuse this question with the question, "How much money do you *want*?" Want and need are two very different things.

So, how much money do you *need*?

Knowing how much money you *actually* need, compared to how much you *think* you need, or how much money you're *used to* having, is empowering. Suddenly you have all kinds of options.

Now, I could go ahead and ask you how much money you want, but the answer to that question is inevitably "A lot!" So instead, we're going to talk about *value*.

Think of your job as an energy exchange. You give your employer your time and talents, and they give you money in exchange. How do you feel about that exchange? Are you getting a good deal? Some people love their jobs so much that it feels like highway robbery. *You mean I get paid to do this?!* Other people feel like they're getting the shitty end of the stick. *This is sooooo not worth it.*

This energy exchange includes not only time and money, but also emotional and psychological energy in the form of things like worry, satisfaction, stress, happiness, exhaustion, fulfillment, etc.

So, is what you're putting into your job worth what you're getting out of it? Are you getting good value in this energy exchange? Does it feel like highway robbery, the shitty end of the stick, or somewhere in between?

If your job feels like highway robbery, you've got an awesome gig that gives you wonderful value! Stop reading this right now and go off and enjoy your life!

If your job feels not quite like highway robbery, but not quite like the shitty end of the stick, some tweaks are necessary. You're not exactly getting a sour deal, but you're not getting a fantastic one either. Some changes might be called for.

If you consistently feel like you're getting the shitty end of the stick at work, an overhaul is needed. What you're putting into your work just isn't worth it. You could do better. Nobody wants to get the shitty end of the stick.

Is what you're putting into your job worth what you're getting out of it?

WHO'S
THE BOSS?

A lot of people have a slave/master relationship with money. And you know who's usually in charge? Money.

Without ever intending to, and often without even noticing, people become slaves to money. I've seen people pursue entrepreneurship specifically because they wanted more freedom, only to drive themselves into the ground with 70-hour workweeks, hustling for more and more cash. I've also seen very successful, very wealthy people scrape and scramble for even more money.

People spend what they have. If you make more money, you spend more money, and then you have to hustle for more to keep up with your lifestyle. There are a lot of people out there who have a great lifestyle on paper — beautiful properties, expensive sports cars, gorgeous vacation homes — only they never get to actually enjoy their so-called lifestyle because they don't have a life. They're always at work, hustling for their paycheck, grinding out their days chained to their desk, feeding the machine.

That doesn't actually sound like a glamorous lifestyle after all, does it? For people like this (and perhaps for you), the question becomes, *Who's the boss, you or your money?* In other words, are you working for your money, or is it working for you? Not sure? Answer this question instead: Is your money helping you cash in on happiness, or is the work you have to do to earn it leaving your spirit poor?

Who's the boss, you or your money?

Let's say the work you do for your money is leaving your spirit poor. What then?

A really obvious solution is to make your money doing different work — work that doesn't leave your spirit poor. Another solution — a complementary one, and one that is rarely considered — is to decide *how* you want your money to work for you. What is it you *want* from your money?

If you're a slave to money, and you're not especially

Is your money helping you cash in on happiness, or is the work you have to do to earn it leaving your spirit poor?

pleased with that arrangement, you need to get clear — crystal clear — on what you want your money to do for you. That's how you turn the tables. That's how you take your power back and renegotiate the terms of your agreement: by deciding exactly how you want your money to serve you.

If you're thinking, *Uh, duh. I want my money to pay the bills*, then you're not getting nearly specific enough. Not even close. You need to dictate precisely what you want your money to do for you in exacting detail.

Here, I'll use myself as an example. I want my money to provide me with the following things:

I want to have a warm, welcoming, comfortable home, full of good vibes. This means furniture, art, and objects I adore. Size doesn't matter much to me. It's more about the energy of the space.

I want the freedom to choose how I spend my days. For me, that means running my own business and also not overfilling my schedule. I want a couple of days a week to do whatever the hell I want.

I want to express my fun, quirky style with things like clothing, accessories, and even stationery and decor. These little details bring me an insane amount of joy.

I'm a worrier by nature, so I want to have a large enough financial cushion that I don't have to worry about the immediate future.

I want to explore beautiful places, go outside, stroll,

hang out in cool cafes, and enjoy art. I don't need much money for this, but I do need time.

I want delicious, nourishing meals that I don't always have to make myself. That means spending a little more than the average bear at hip, healthy restaurants.

Now, it turns out that a certain amount of money will easily provide me with all of those things — and it's not all that much. I can have everything I want without needing a giant, bloated paycheck. Even a moderate amount is more than enough, plus a comfortable cushion. Do you have any idea how empowering this is for a generally fretful, worrisome control freak like me? Once I decided exactly how I wanted my money to serve me, I was no longer at the mercy of "more." More is certainly nice, but knowing you can have exactly what you want without it is incredibly liberating.

Now you try. What do you want your money to do for you? What are the most important things to you?

Maybe you want enough to cover the expenses of starting a family.

Maybe you want to pay off your student debt in the next two years.

Maybe you'd love to put your kids through private school.

Maybe there's a month-long vacation you'd like to take.

Maybe you'd like to put a down payment on a house.

Maybe you have more than you need, and you just want to get your new business up and running.

Maybe you really have a thing for designer shoes, and you'd like to treat yourself from time to time.

Once you're really clear on what you want from your money (and *why* you want it . . . remember *enlightened ambition*?), you can get your money working for you again. You know that enough is enough and the rest is gravy. That sure puts you in charge again. Anything you can do to loosen money's grip on you gives you more freedom in your career. Take your power back.

FAILURE

THE ONLY PLACE WHERE THERE IS NO
RISK OF FAILURE IS ON THE SIDELINES —
AND THAT'S NOT WHERE YOU WANT TO BE.

WORST-CASE
SCENARIO

We've talked about irrational doomsday bag lady fears, but what about the real-life worst-case scenarios?

Don't think about that! some will say. *It's negative energy! Leap and the net will appear! When you fall, you fly! Do what you love and the money will follow!*

A part of me would love to embrace the whole "trust the universe" thing, but another part of me thinks, *Are you fucking kidding me? Not a chance in hell.*

This part — the healthy skeptic — is a part I recommend you consult with before you go gung ho. Your healthy skeptic isn't going to freak out and convince you that you'll be living in a dumpster if you don't stay on your current career trajectory — but it *will* bring your attention to potential risks and pitfalls, including the worst-case scenario.

I happen to think that getting a good, clear picture of your worst-case scenario — the one that's within the realm of possibility if your plan goes to hell in a handbasket — is a very, *very* good thing. Because what happens in the unfortunate event that your plan *does* go to hell in a handbasket? You need to know what that scenario looks like, and you need to know it in advance, so you can decide if the risk is worth taking.

> Getting a good, clear picture of your worst-case scenario — the one that's within the realm of possibility if your plan goes to hell in a handbasket — is a very, *very* good thing.

If you take out a second mortgage to fund your business, you and your family might lose your home if it all goes to shit. That might not be a risk worth taking. I sure as hell wouldn't take it. If your worst-case scenario will

We almost
always fail
to calculate
the risk
of **NOT**
taking action.

leave you in dire straits, you might want to consider taking smaller risks and making your transition more gradual. Smaller bites. On the other hand, if your worst-case scenario is just a bruised ego or moving on to Plan B, is that really so bad? Your worst-case scenario will be different depending on the risk, your contingency plan, your support system, and your safety net.

I was terrified I might crash and burn when I first thought of leaving my career path in academia to start my own business, so you bet your ass I took a good hard look at the potential fallout before I made my move. I looked it right in the eye. I didn't have a lot of money in the bank, so living off a big, juicy nest egg for a while wasn't an option. If my business ended in miserable failure, I'd have to pick up a couple of teaching contracts (work I actually enjoyed), go back to one of my old jobs, or find a new one. That wouldn't be so bad. Sure, I'd have to deal with the disappointment, but I'd still be able to live comfortably.

Looking at your worst-case scenario is empowering. It helps you determine whether a risk is worth taking. For me, it was. For many, it is. Take a look at your own worst-case scenario. Go there. Go there, but don't *stay* there. Stay there and you'll talk yourself out of ever taking action. Looking at your worst-case scenario is simply an exercise in calculating risk so you can make a good decision for yourself, whether it means moving forward or adjusting your plans accordingly.

If you're going to look at the worst-case scenario for taking action toward the thing you want to do, you should also explore the worst-case scenario for *not* taking action. What are the risks of not making a change, of not trying something new, of not setting out on your own, of not quitting something you hate? We naturally look at risk when we think of taking action, but we almost always fail to calculate the risk of *not* taking action. Doing nothing is risky, too, and — depending on the current state of your health and happiness — it's often far riskier.

THE AGONY
OF DEFEAT

Let's say you muster the guts to really put yourself out there, but you don't book the interview, land the client, make the cut, get the gig.

Rejection sucks. Especially when you go out on a limb and go after what you want . . . and then you don't get it. Yes, you knew there was a chance you'd get burned, but the possibility and the reality are two different things. Fear of failure exists only in your mind. Actual failure exists in real life, where you can feel it and where other people can see it. You ask yourself, *What will people think?* There may be embarrassment. There may be shame. The agony of defeat is just that — an agonizing, miserable blow.

So what do you do when you put yourself out there and you don't get what you want?

Well, first you take a moment to deal with the dashed hopes and the heartbreak. You process. You swear. You cry. You go for a long, angry run. You buy yourself a tub of cookie dough ice cream. You're kind and gentle with yourself. You take your time.

Then you try again.

You take your magic, and you cast it elsewhere. Rework it. Refine it. Breathe new life into it. Then you telepathically invite your dissers to fuck off. Or you decide to send them light and love. Your choice. Their loss.

Getting rejected is a part of life. When it happens to you (and I say *when*, not if), it means you're out there trying to make things happen. It's a small consolation, but it counts for something.

The truth is, you probably won't get exactly what you want on the very first try. That's not how it works. Did you know that books like *Harry Potter*, *Animal Farm*, *The Alchemist*, and *Chicken Soup for the Soul* all got rejected by publishers on the first try — and, in one case, on the 10th, 11th, and even 12th try? (That was *Harry Potter*. I bet those publishers are kicking themselves now.) If people like J.K. Rowling and George Orwell had to give it another shot, what makes the rest of us think we're exempt from having to try again?

When a door slams in your face it's tempting to just throw your hands up and say, *Well, fuck it*. But don't forget you can always try again. Maybe the timing isn't right. Maybe you need a different strategy. Just because a door is closed doesn't mean it's closed forever.

If you ask someone out on a date, there is always a chance they'll say no. If you say "I love you" for the first time, there is always a chance that you won't hear it back. If you ask someone to marry you, you can't be 100 percent sure that they'll say yes. You hope so (especially if there is a Jumbotron involved), but you never know. People risk the excruciating vulnerability of putting themselves out there all the time. Why? Because *what if*? What if you get the date? What if they love you too? What if they say yes? The risk is worth it.

Just because a door is closed doesn't mean it's closed forever.

True, you might not get the raise. You might not get the job interview. You might not get the promotion, even if you think you're a shoo-in. Your business might not take off the way you want it to. But *what if*? What if you *do* get the raise? What if you *do* get the job interview? What if you *do* get the promotion? What if your business *does* take off exactly as you hoped it would? Might be worth trying, right?

The only place where there is no risk of failure is on the sidelines — and that's not where you want to be.

PLAN B

It feels awful to grasp after something that just isn't working — a business that is failing, studies you no longer like, a career path that is leading you in the wrong direction — but it's also hard to let go. Letting go usually involves embracing Plan B, and embracing Plan B is hard to do.

Plan B means that Plan A didn't work out. It wasn't quite right. But what's worse: moving on to something else, or staying with something that isn't right? I'll take moving on, *thankyouverymuch*.

My entire career has been a series of Plan Bs. Indeed, *most* people's careers have been a series of Plan Bs, Cs, and Ds. People born after the baby boom years hold an average of 12 jobs in their 20s, 30s, and 40s, and 15 jobs (*fifteen*!)

What was so great about PLAN A, anyway?

throughout their lifetime. You're certainly not alone in moving on to Plan B.

Plus, any change you've ever made, aside from anything you've calculated from the very beginning, has been a Plan B. Think about that the next time you find yourself resisting Plan B. You've already gone there. Life is better there, and you can go there again.

Let's take a look at my career, shall we? When I was a teenager, a very well-intentioned guidance counselor suggested I should become a journalist. I knew I loved writing, so I thought, *journalist it is*. I got a journalism degree from the best school in the country and proceeded to live happily ever after. THE END.

Just kidding. I didn't like journalism, so never I became a journalist. I had a shiny degree to hang on the wall, but no idea what to do next. Time for Plan B. At that time, Plan B meant working full-time hours at my crappy part-time retail job at a store that sold eyebrow rings and psychedelic candles. I wore platform boots and a lot of eyeliner. I didn't know exactly what I wanted yet, but I knew it wasn't a promising career selling facial jewelry, and so I quietly plotted for the next Plan B, which was to get a "real, grown-up job."

I got a four-month contract working as a university recruiter, something I had zero training in and had never planned to do. And I friggin' *loved* it! I told my boss I wanted to stay, and I worked for her for another six years, slowly taking on bigger projects and more responsibility.

I got promoted a handful of times until I was managing a team in a brand new area. That role taught me a lot, but I soon felt bored. I wasn't growing anymore, and I didn't want my boss's job or a job like it. It was time to think up another Plan B.

I did a master's degree in business and liked it so much that I thought I might like to do a Ph.D. So I quit my job and dove headfirst into academia. I liked the coursework, but the minute we started conducting research, I knew it wasn't for me. To cope with my hatred for conducting research, I focused on teaching instead. I taught a couple of courses for a few semesters and was eventually hired to design a course of my own. It was awesome, but it was also a happy distraction from doing my research. While I loved teaching, I hated research, and so deep down I knew the life of a professor wasn't for me. Time for another Plan B.

I got some coach training and started building my coaching practice while I was still working as a prof. I love love *loved* the coaching work. My new plan was to finish my Ph.D. and then move full-time into the coaching practice. The problem was that I *reeeeeally* hated doing research. Forcing myself to finish my dissertation felt like torture. This time I fought Plan B. Hard. I knew I'd be much happier if I just quit. I didn't want a career in academia anyway, but quitting my Ph.D. 93 pages into my dissertation certainly wasn't a part of The Plan. When I finally decided to quit, I felt instantly better. Like, *instantly*, the very minute I gave notice, even though I would continue to teach for four more months. Plan B was my light at the end of the tunnel.

Thank goodness I embraced Plan B because life is so much better now. My work is wonderful, and as a result my whole life is happier. Every tweak and turn has been just another Plan B, and I'll be happily (or unhappily, depending on my level of resistance) Plan B–ing for the rest of my life . . . along with every other human on the planet.

The thought of moving to Plan B feels awful at first . . . until it doesn't. Somewhere along the way, Plan B starts to feel empowering, and it fits way better, and you start to wonder, *What was so great about Plan A, anyway?* People grow. Interests change. Who you were when you made Plan A might not be who you are now. If Plan A doesn't work, or if it's no longer what you want, there are another 25 letters behind it. Use them. Goodness knows, I've got half of the alphabet scattered across my career path.

> People grow. Interests change.
> Who you were when you made
> Plan A might not be who
> you are now.

DON'T
APOLOGIZE

I ran into an acquaintance just after she'd taken a meeting about some freelance copywriting work for her new business, so I asked her how the business was doing.

"Good, I guess," she said, shrugging and casting her eyes downward. "I mean, I'm still doing some other stuff to supplement my income."

She was pretty sheepish about the whole thing. It seemed like she was embarrassed or ashamed — apologetic, even — about needing to take on other work while making her career transition.

I see this a lot. And I get it. I *sooooo* get it. It's not awesome to have to take on other work because you're trying to break into a new field, or because your new business isn't making enough money to pay the bills. Yet most people — myself included — do this in the beginning of a new career chapter. I kept my gig as a professor for a while before I took my business full-time. Success doesn't happen overnight.

Not being psyched about your transition work is one thing; feeling ashamed of it is another. You needn't feel insecure about doing what you have to do to pay the rent and put food in mouths while you get things off the ground. Don't apologize for the hustle. OWN it.

Holding down a waitressing job so you can be available for auditions? OWN it. You're doing what you have to do to make your chosen profession work.

> # Don't apologize for the hustle. OWN it.

Still working trade shows while you're looking for a gig in public relations? OWN it. Trade shows are a good way to meet people, anyway.

Working part-time at a retail job while you write your book? OWN it. You're getting paid to think up your next chapter title while folding sweaters.

Working full-time for a bank to pay off your debt

while secretly building your own business on evenings and weekends? OWN it. Who wants to start a business in debt, anyway?

I have a friend who works as a waitress to supplement her work in musical theatre. One of my clients works full-time for a start-up to fund her growing media consulting business. Another is still working as a social worker while she builds her counseling practice. A colleague takes a few hours at a retail gig to supplement her business income. As you know, my brother worked as a math tutor while breaking into television writing. People do what they have to do.

Let's remove the cloak of shame around the various ways we make money.

You can either frame this kind of work as a joe job, something that is beneath you, or you can choose to think of it as the very thing that lets you chase the dream. It's the safety net, the scaffolding that supports you as you build what's next. Framing matters, and the only person who can frame how you think about your work is you.

Making a career change is a daring and delicate thing, so let's remove the cloak of shame around the various ways we make money. You have to start somewhere, and every person who has ever built something or made a big change started with something small. You are not a second-rate professional just because you're embarking on your second career (or your third, or fourth — or tenth, for that matter).

All of this stuff takes time, not to mention guts and hard work. Despite what you've heard, life is not a race. You'll get there eventually. In the meantime, you're doing what you need to do to build The Dream. Don't apologize for it. Not ever.

EVERYBODY'S
TWO CENTS

THERE ARE FOUR LITTLE WORDS THAT CAN
REALLY FUCK THINGS UP FOR US WHEN WE'RE
AT AN IMPORTANT CAREER CROSSROADS:
WHAT WILL PEOPLE THINK?

WHAT
WILL PEOPLE THINK?

Let's say you've done the hard work of getting honest with yourself about what you really want. First of all — congratulations! Seriously. Do you have any idea how many people never commit to figuring out what they want and end up slogging away at stuff they don't like for their entire lives? Figuring out what you want is a HUGE accomplishment.

But what if the work you want to do isn't exactly, you know, impressive? Or traditional? Or prestigious? Or super lucrative? Or what your family or teachers or mentors wanted you to do? What if it looks like a step backward to some people? Or seems like a huge, random departure from what you were doing before? What if it's unconventional, or even a little bit weird?

There are four little words that can really fuck things up for us when we're at an important career crossroads: *What will people think?*

That question can send people off the rails and right back to where they started. The minute we start worrying about what people will think, we get all wrapped up in ego. Your ego (and my ego, everybody's ego) is the social acceptance rule police. It's like the spazzy clique of hot, popular girls from the movie *Mean Girls* — if you forget to wear pink on Wednesdays, or, heaven forbid, if you wear sweatpants, you can't sit with the cool kids. Those are the rules.

One of my clients, Adam, was really hung up on what his two sets of friends would think about his career decisions. He had a set of hippie friends and a set of yuppie friends. If he worked in business, he feared he'd get flak from his hippie friends. If he worked in the arts, he thought his yuppie friends would look down on him. He was worrying about what everyone else thought and giving away all of his power. Adam was afraid the cool kids wouldn't let him sit with them anymore.

If you're like Adam and you're afraid some of your social circle will abandon you because of your career, you are hangin' with the wrong crowd, my friend. You are going to drive yourself nuts with crazy hypotheticals that may or may not happen (and in my experience, almost never happen).

Another client, Jo, was jazzed about finance. She happily envisioned her future career — her office, her colleagues,

Some people aren't going to get it, and that's okay.

and even what shoes she would wear. I would rather eat a solid diet of cat food than work in finance. Had I expressed this to Jo (which obviously I didn't), she would have been right to totally disregard my opinion, and any similar opinions from others, and keep on truckin'. It's *her* life.

Don't make your decisions contingent on an endorsement, a seal of approval, or a pat on the back from everyone in your life. Because honey, it ain't gonna happen. Some people aren't going to get it, and that's okay. No sense in worrying about it before you even make your move.

If you're stressing out about what the people around you will think about your decisions, you probably haven't done enough work to get comfortable with your decisions yourself. I know this because it took me years of misery and a very public breakdown to get over my own fears of what people would think about my career change.

I had to strip away a bunch of shitty stories I was telling myself — stories about a never-ending list of things I had to do in order to be accepted, which included slogging it out and proving my worth again and again and again. I have been a high-striving, high-stress go-getter for a long time. I look damn good on paper. I'm used to the fleeting euphoria that comes with accolades and praise, always followed by grasping after the Next Big Thing. Worrying about what people think is exhausting and (thank goodness I finally realized it) totally not worth it.

When you strip it right down, the question *What will people think?* really has nothing to do with other people and everything to do with *you* — your desire to be accepted, your approval hang-ups, your need to be liked. I know it's not just me.

You know what my dad said when I told him I was leaving academia? He said, "I'm proud of you." Those were the first words out of his mouth. He knew I was miserable, and at the end of the day he just wanted me to be happy. Sometimes the only voices of disapproval are the ones inside our own heads.

The question
What will people think?
really has nothing to
do with other people and
everything to do with *you.*

WHERE
IS THE PARADE I ORDERED?

Let's say you know what you want for your career, and you've finally worked up the nerve to tell people about it. You have an awesome crew, and you know they're going to be just as psyched as you are. Bring. It. On. There ought to be a parade in your honor because you are about to make some really amazing shit happen.

You excitedly share your big news with the people you care about, but instead of a parade you get . . . crickets. Or worse, you get a random subject change to a mundane and totally unrelated topic. All you want is a high five, or a hug — or at the very least a fist bump — but everybody leaves you hangin'.

Here are some of the weird reactions and non-reactions you might get from family, friends, and colleagues when you share the exciting news about your desired career path:

RADIO SILENCE

Radio silence is awkward as hell. The news of your new career path has become a record-screeching, everybody-stop-and-stare, broken-glass-in-the-background conversation stopper. At the most, you might get a surprised "oh," followed by a blank stare.

PRESTO CHANGE-O

You tried to share your career news, but somehow you ended up in a conversation about your cousin's cat that pukes on the radiator. The person you're talking to bulldozed right over your big reveal with a polite nod, followed by a subject change from left field. You didn't see it coming.

PITY PARTY

Ugh. This is the Debbie Downer of reactions. In less than three seconds flat, your exciting news has become one big sad trombone, and your landlady/sister-in-law/payroll supervisor/coworker from hell is coming apart at the seams. *Oh, I wish I could do that. You're so lucky. My life sucks.* You're confused because you thought this was about you and not them, but apparently you were wrong. You selfish jerk.

JUDGY WUDGY

You can hear the condescending air quotes in her voice. *Oh isn't that "precious,"* she'll say. *I hope you enjoy your "little project."* Or maybe she'll dish out some passive-aggressive "must be nice" comments. *Must be nice to have alllll that time on your hands.* Resist the urge to snap her like a Kit Kat bar and run her over with her own minivan. After an encounter with Judgy Wudgy, I recommend you go straight home, lock the door, pull down the shades, and break something.

> # The thing nobody tells you about getting happy is that it can be kind of lonely at first.

You know that tuba sound on *The Price Is Right* when there's a new car or oven range or pair of Jet Skis on the line, and the person *doesn't* win all the fabulous merchandise? That's what it can feel like when you finally share your news with someone you care about, and you get one of these reactions.

The thing nobody tells you about getting happy is that it can be kind of lonely at first, which is really weird because all you want to do is share your happiness and excitement with the people you love. Some of your peeps will be psyched for you and give you a pat on the back, or a punch on the shoulder — or, if you're really lucky, one of those sorority sister squealy jump-for-joy hugs — but not everyone will.

What? You're going to be a life coach? A brew master? A chef? Um, okay. Some people might not know what to say. Or maybe they're feeling a little envy, and they don't want to say too much. It can be incredibly painful to watch somebody make a change that you want to make yourself. Some of your weirdest reactions will come from people who wish they were making some changes of their own.

ANGELS
AND ASSHOLES

There are probably people in your life who just won't get in your corner. They push you in the opposite direction you want to go. They tell you to pick the safe thing, go the traditional route, be sensible, stay the course, grow up, and get serious.

They know your soul is screaming at you to do something different, but they just won't have it. They shoot down your plans and act like pushy jerks about decisions that really have nothing to do with them. Assholes.

Your colleague says, "I know you want to quit your corporate job and start your own business, but you'll never be able to make a living."

Your dad says, "I know you want to study literature, but if you go to med school instead, I'll pay for it."

Your teacher says, "It's wonderful that you love music, but music is more of a hobby. You should study business, so you'll have something to fall back on."

Your friend says, "Making a career change this late in the game is a pretty stupid move."

Why can't these people just be supportive and stop acting like assholes, already? I have a theory, and it's this: They're not assholes; they're scared humans.

Maybe you're getting pushback from people like this — the people you respect and care about most. Of course your father and your sister and your best friend and your partner want what's best for you. Here's what they're really saying when they're acting like unsupportive assholes:

I don't want you to fail.

I want to protect you.

I don't want you to get hurt.

I want you to be okay.

These are scared human thoughts. These loving curmudgeons are just scared for you and want the very best for you. Unfortunately, this does not make them good counsel for your career choices. You may need to put a little distance between yourself and anyone who is being unnecessarily harsh. You don't have to cut ties with people you love; keep loving them, but do not give your power away.

And while you're at it, build yourself a team of benevolent supporters — a team of career navigation angels. You want people who are going to lift you up, people who will be supportive, guiding influencers, people who are in your corner, people who inspire and support you. These people are going to help you get from where you are to where you want to be. If you're lucky, you probably already have some people like this around you.

Remember how in gym class, you got to be the team captain occasionally? You and some other kid each got to pick a team, member by member. You made careful decisions about who you picked for your team because you wanted to win the game. You chose people who you thought would help you do that. Life is like that, too. You're the captain, and you get to pick your team.

Your team might include friends, family members, colleagues, mentors, and acquaintances. Some of them might be people you don't even know yet, like someone you contact out of the blue to ask for advice or guidance. Or they might be people you'll never actually meet — people who've written books or blogs, made videos, or given talks and workshops.

Your team members may come in many shapes and sizes. Seek out people you sense are going to lift you up and help you move forward. Who inspires you? Who challenges you to grow? Who makes you feel strong? Those are the people you want on your team. Learn from them and lean on them to help you get where you want to go.

Your angels and assholes are, weirdly, equally loving — they just show their love in *very* different ways. Those ways have nothing to do with you and everything to do with them, their own fears, and their own ways of looking at the world. Once you understand that, an asshole doesn't look all that different from an angel. They all care about you, but *you're* the captain. Remember that as you assemble your team.

You're the captain, and you get to pick your team.

WATCH
YOUR LANGUAGE

Like your mother said, *Watch your language!* What you say about your choices matters. This includes your internal dialogue.

I have a client who chose to stay at her government job for an extra year so she could save up some cash to start her own business. Security was important to her, and doing it that way — building a big financial cushion before she started — made her feel safe. The thought of jumping without a safety net gave her hives, so she came up with a plan that felt good. Slow and steady.

She told me about her freedom plan, and then she said, "I guess I'll just have to suck it up for a year."

"Now hold it right there, lady," I said. "You just came up with a kickass plan to build a business in a way that feels good to you. Does it really feel like you're sucking it up?"

"No," she said. "But you know what I mean."

The language she used to describe her decision to keep her job for the next year — "sucking it up" — took the wind out of her sails, so we worked on a reframe. She came up with "I'm choosing to stay in my job for another year, so I can fund The Dream."

OWN your choices.
Claim them. Stand in them.

Doesn't that sound better than sucking it up?

Sucking it up feels shitty. It makes you feel powerless, victimized, and defeated. *Choosing* something, and really owning it, comes from a much more empowered place. Small shift, big difference.

OWN your choices. Claim them. Stand in them. Using defeated language, even if it's just to yourself, will only make you feel — you guessed it — defeated.

Now, language alone isn't going to cut it if you're lying to yourself.

If your job crushes your soul and you have no exit plan, all the flowery language in the world isn't going to make you feel good about it. In fact, flowery language will probably make you feel *worse*. Lying to yourself always feels bad. I think that's why some people have trouble with affirmations. For many, they feel like empty words projecting fake optimism.

Can't find any authentic positive language to frame your choices? Then your problem isn't your language; it's your choices. And there's only one solution for that: stop making choices that feel shitty.

BEGINNING

EMBRACE YOUR INNER AMATEUR.

MAKE
ROOM

I recently got rid of about 20 percent of the crap in my closet. And it felt fan-fucking-tastic! Included in the purge: every pair of high heels that hurt my feet, anything beige, a briefcase that I hated, and pretty lace underwear that I loved but was too small. Because, really, who needs a daily reminder that your ass used to be smaller?

That crap was bringing me down. Harshing my mellow. Killing my vibe. So I got rid of it.

Next, I took to my bathroom. That designer perfume that made me sneeze? Gone. Same for the expensive face cream that made my face look like Exxon Valdez. Goodbye to all of the ugly makeup that any MAC or Clinique lady ever talked me into.

I also ditched about a gazillion books, including one by a wise spiritual leader that I've tried to read about a hundred times but just. can't. get. into. So much for enlightenment. But I did keep my collection of *O Magazine* back issues. Because nobody fucks with Oprah. Plus, I need those to make vision boards. Obviously.

After four trips to the donation bin and one to the garbage chute, I felt so much better. Lighter. I found permanent homes for the stacks of stuff that were cluttering the kitchen table without having to Tetris them into already bulging shelves. I made room for my high-school yearbooks. And for books I wrote as a kid (complete with homemade cereal-box-and-wallpaper covers). I made space to actually *see* the lovely things I already have, and room for things I don't have yet. My vision is no longer cluttered with stuff I don't even like.

So why am I telling you all of this?

This isn't about my closet or my shelves. This is about making room. In your career. In your life.

If you're unhappy with your career (or, indeed, your closet or shelves), you need to make space. You need to clear the decks and let go of some of the things that are getting in your way — the epic time suck, the shitty obligations, the stuff that is weighing you down and cramping your style. That's the stuff that is standing between you and what you want.

Time and space and energy are not infinite. If you want

something to come into your life — more time, greater health, a better job, your own business, you name it — you have to make room for it. Get rid of some of the stuff that isn't serving you anymore. Start saying no more often, so that you can say yes when you really *want* to.

Maybe that means you leave the office at a reasonable hour (gasp!). Maybe that means you ask for a little more help (okay, a *lot* more help) from your spouse. Maybe that means you cool it with the Supermom/dad thing for a while. Maybe that means you cut out some of your kids' after-school activities (they'll survive), and bring store-bought cookies to the friggin' PTA bake sale. Maybe that means you switch to part-time studies. Maybe that means you're not the office all-star this quarter. Maybe that means you don't scarf your lunch hunched over your desk. Maybe that means you go for a hike instead of taking a meeting. You get to choose what stays and what goes, but *some* of it must go if you want something more in your life.

Time and space and energy are not infinite. If you want something to come into your life, you have to make room for it.

Make room. Make room for all of the good stuff you want in your life. Because it won't show up if you don't have room for it.

AMATEUR

I recently watched a little boy teach his father how to dribble a basketball. The boy was about eight years old, and it was clear that his father had never even held a basketball, let alone played a game. He held his arm out at a rigid 90 degrees and slapped the ball at shoulder height with a flat, open palm. A few wobbly bounces in, the ball veered off into the bushes.

"Like this," the boy said. "Do it lower to the ground." He passed the ball to his father. "Hmmm. Try bending your elbow more. Yes. That's better."

The ball spiked off to the bushes again within seconds. The boy retrieved it, and they tried again.

"It will help if you bend your knees a little bit. Here, I'll show you."

And on it went. It seemed like such a tender father–son moment. I admired the father. He and his son were in the courtyard of my building — such a public place — and I saw no shame or embarrassment in him as his young boy taught him this simple skill. Such humility. He was just learning.

Why do we assume that we should be good at something right from the get-go? And why do we freak out when we aren't? It's like we've forgotten the important step of *learning*. All that self-imposed pressure to get it right the first time, to be an expert, the best of the best — it's debilitating. No wonder we're afraid to jump into something new. We feel like failures if it's not a slam dunk on the first try.

When you're the grown-up, expert, or authority on something, you're used to knowing your shit inside out. A willingness to learn something new doesn't come easy.

Yeah, but I don't know anything about that.

Yeah, but I've already worked for 15 years in this field. I'll have to start all over.

Yeah, but that means I'll have to go back to school.

Yeah, but I'm an expert in this
and I'll only be a novice at that.

Of course we want to be good at the things we pursue, but getting there requires a willingness to take the first shaky step, even if it means starting with the basics, risking looking stupid, asking dumb questions, or learning from someone much younger than yourself — like, say, an eight-year-old kid.

Nobody ever nails it the first time.

A colleague of mine, Maya, wanted to start her own business and sought me out for advice. She was smart and full of ideas and had a solid plan, but she felt paralyzed. She was bogged down in fear. When I asked her what her biggest, most troubling fear was, she took a deep, bracing breath and said, "I'm afraid I'm going to do it wrong."

"Here's the thing . . ." I said. She cut me off before I could finish.

"It's impossible to do it wrong, right?" she said. "Is that what you're going to say?"

"Actually no," I said. "I was going to say the opposite. It's impossible *not* to get it wrong on the first try. I did. And I have two graduate degrees in business, and I used to teach at a business school. If anyone should have nailed it the first time, it's me. But *nobody* ever nails it the first time. Neither will you."

Maya's shoulders relaxed. She looked relieved. This always happens when I talk to people about the inevitability of making mistakes. Knowing that you're going to get some of it wrong on the first try (and that everyone else does, too) actually takes the edge off. The fear is no longer paralyzing, and we can lose some of the shame around not being perfect right out of the gate.

Trying is step 1 in getting it right. Trying again is step 2.

Attempting anything new, whether it's starting your own business, making a career change, or, hell, even learning to dribble a basketball, puts you in the vulnerable position of having to learn something new. This is when you have to embrace your inner amateur — the part of you that is willing to try for the hope of becoming better.

Learning something new takes guts, especially when it's very likely that you'll suck at it in the beginning. Trying is step 1 in getting it right. Trying again is step 2.

The good news is, being an amateur is temporary. Kind of. You learn a little about something you knew nothing about, and suddenly you're less of an amateur. Keep working on it, and you may become a pro. Really hone your skills, and you may eventually reach the level of mastery. But eventually, you'll want to try something in a new area, something you know nothing about, and so you'll become an amateur once again. Embrace it. Or, if you can't find the willingness to embrace it, at least don't fight it. Who knows what you might learn?

GLAMOROUS, IT'S NOT

It's not glamorous to learn how to dribble a basketball from your eight-year-old kid. It's not glamorous to fumble your way through a job interview in a totally new field. Or to stammer through your first pitch meeting. Or to try to write a cover letter when you haven't written one for 20 years. Or when you give your first keynote speech, and you can't get the goddamn PowerPoint clicky thingy to work.

You know why it's not glamorous? Because nobody knows what the hell they're doing when they're trying something new. We're like newborn elephants learning to walk for the first time and tripping over our own trunks. It's sweet as hell, but not graceful.

But some people naturally radiate grace, you say. *I want to be like* those *people, the people who make it look exciting and glamorous, and effortless to boot.*

Those people had to start somewhere too, you know. We forget that. And do you know how those people got to be so good at what they do? They tried some stuff, made a bunch of mistakes, learned from their mistakes, and got better with practice — just like anybody who ever did anything. We're talking Oprah, Adele, Beyoncé, and all those chicks you follow on Instagram who really seem to have their shit together.

Some things
— like breast symmetry —
just don't matter when
you're getting shit done.

People like to romanticize the life of a writer. *There's so much freedom to just write all day! And shopping for a publisher and throwing a launch party must be so glamorous!* I'm pretty new to this club, but none of the writers I know are sneezing rainbows or shitting glitter. They're working away on their projects just like everyone else. I'm currently writing this from a drafty studio in a no-frills building that used to be an old schoolhouse. The underwire on the left side of my bra fell out earlier today. I'm wearing the same sweatpants as yesterday and typing feverishly as my unsupported left boob hangs an inch lower than my right one. Did I mention I'm staying here all week, and I only brought one bra? Oh well. Some things — like breast symmetry — just don't matter when you're getting shit done. Glamorous, it's not.

Entrepreneurship also gets overglamorized. Many of the entrepreneurs I know work way more hours now than they did at their old jobs. Still, there's a common perception that it's all glitz and glam, übercreativity, traveling the world, and laptops at the beach. Here are some of the not-so-glamorous things I encountered when starting my business:

- I spent an entire 10-hour workday learning to embed tweetable links into 40 blog posts. Zzzz . . .
- I rewrote my "About" page 10 effing times. That sucker is hard to get right. Still haven't nailed it.
- Every week, I had to cross-post a piece of writing to four different blogging platforms, all with totally different publishing technology. It took me longer to publish my stuff than to write it.
- I recorded and edited my own videos: quick confirmation for how unglamorous I am. Seriously. Try it. You'll cover all the mirrors with butcher

paper and cringe at the sound of your own voice for at least a week.

- I spent umpteen hours gathering and posting client testimonials. Do you have any idea how awkward it is to ask someone to tell you how awesome you are? And then ask them to put it in writing?
- I spent several hours every week just answering emails. If there's a job out there that doesn't involve email, I haven't found it yet.

Are you sleeping yet? Who could blame you? That shit is boring as hell. So is a decent chunk of the stuff you'll find in any line of work — even your dream job. Definitely make the career changes you want, but adjust any expectations you may have about it being all champagne and fireworks. The beginning of anything is *especially* unglamorous. There's not likely to be streamers and confetti as you make your transition (unless you become a party planner, in which case you'll come to hate streamers and confetti). And if you *do* start sneezing rainbows or shitting glitter, I recommend you call a doctor.

GET
IN THE GAME

Things are pretty comfortable when you're watching from the sidelines. Up there on the bleachers, you're a safe distance from the battlefield. You've got your blanket, some snacks, and, if you're smart, one of those squishy bum cushions. You get to live vicariously and feel like you're a part of the action, all while sitting on your ass. The people out there, they're giving blood and sweat and tears. They've got skin in the game, and you've got . . . nachos.

But what if you don't really want to be watching from the sidelines? What if you'd rather be out on the field making things happen? Hanging out on the bleachers eating nachos suddenly isn't all that appealing.

Watching from the sidelines when you'd rather be in the game is what I call living in the "wish zone." This is where a lot of people live when it comes to their career. Even people who fully intend to get in the game one day, but never actually *do* it.

Watching from a distance can be a great thing to do when you're getting the lay of the land. You can learn some of the rules and check out everybody's moves, but there's only so much you can soak up from the sidelines. Eventually, you're going to get hungry. Not hungry for nachos (goodness knows, you've got plenty of those), but hungry for *action*. You're ready to get out there and MAKE. SHIT. HAPPEN.

Here's what I consider the secret formula for making shit happen:

GUTS

+

KNOW-HOW

+

SWEAT

That's it. Those are the three magical ingredients you'll need if you want to get in the game.

Guts means you're willing to take a risk. The surest bet and safest option doesn't sway you from taking some calculated risks that might pay off big. Nobody who plays it safe 100 percent of the time ever got a touchdown, scored the winning goal, or nailed a three-pointer from half-court at the buzzer to win the game.

Depending on what you want, a calculated risk might look like turning down a promotion that isn't right for you, quitting your job and starting your own business, reducing your hours so you can build something on the side, making a lateral move within your company, leaving work for a few years to take care of your young kids, taking a short-term contract gig to get some experience in a new area, or dissolving your small business and reentering the corporate world. All risky moves, but potentially worth it. That's *guts*.

Know-how is a combination of knowledge and skill. You'll be able to pick up some knowledge from the sidelines before you get in the game, but you gain some of it (along with most of your skill) while in play. You may be tempted to stay in knowledge-gathering mode indefinitely, especially if you're an information-gatherer like me. *Just a little more research. Maybe I should take another class. One more book. Okay, two. Or 10.* I never really feel ready. If you're like me, ask yourself, *Do you really need more information or are you just chicken shit?*

Know-how might mean doing an apprenticeship or some volunteer work, taking a class, conducting case studies, going to conferences, working with a mentor or coach, stalking your career idols on the internet to see how they got where they are, joining a mastermind group, or anything else that will help you learn more and sharpen your skills.

Sweat is hard work, pure and simple. If you're taking a risk you hope is going to pay off, you'd better be ready to work for it — because clicking your ruby-slippered heels three times only works for Dorothy. If you tried out for the team (guts) and developed your skills during tryouts (know-how), it makes sense that you'd stick around and work hard at practice (sweat) so you'll be ready for game day, right? Right.

Do you really need more information or are you just chicken shit?

Here's what sweat might look like: Taking a night class after work. Crunching the numbers not once, but three times, to make sure your financials work out. Cutting out your time on social media at work (you know you do it) so you can kick ass on your quarterly presentation. Taking the time to write a beautifully crafted, thoughtful, tailored cover letter for every job you apply for. Actually preparing for your bi-weekly board meeting instead of hoping to fly under the radar or winging it when you get there. Carving out some time to work on your side business even though you still work full-time. Or any number of things that will make you better at what you do (or better at what you *want* to do).

A warning for the perfectionists, burnout crowd, and 150 percenters: Do not confuse pushing yourself to the point of exhaustion with good, healthy, productive sweat. Even Michael Jordan sat on the bench once in a while. Leave a little in the tank for the rest of the game.

The point is to get moving, to get off the bench, out of the "wish zone" and into the game. It's scary and sweaty, but totally worth it because that's where the magic happens. And you can't win if you never find the guts to suit up and play.

AL
DENTE

I boil the shit out of my noodles — probably because I'm an impatient (and therefore absentminded) cook. I figure I can do double duty and get another thing (or 20) done while I'm cooking. This is why I burn everything.

Noodles are hard to burn unless you forget them on the stove and leave your house for several hours — ahem, not that I've done this — but I do regularly overcook them. Noodles that have been overcooked are a slimy, disgusting mess. You're supposed to serve your noodles *al dente*, mostly cooked through but still a little undercooked in the middle.

Maybe we should remember this when we're thinking about doing or making something and putting it out into the world: an idea, a business, a blog post, a piece of art, a plan — it's not supposed to be fully cooked before you serve it up.

Does that make you want to fold over and breathe into a paper bag? Me too. I'm a bit of a control freak, so I like my stuff to be fully cooked — polished and perfect — before I put it out there. The thought of releasing a half-baked idea into the wild makes me want to crawl under the bed.

Hiding under furniture may not be the way to go, but neither is waiting until you iron out all the kinks, cross all the t's, and dot all the i's. You know why? Because you're never going to get there. Not gonna happen. You keep refining and perfecting what you're working on, but it's never done, never flawless, never quite ready, which means you never actually put your work out into the world. If you're constantly doubting your preparedness or over-thinking your next move, here's what you need to know: There comes a point when it's ready *enough*. We just have to learn to recognize when that is. That magic moment will be different depending on the person and the project, but it's almost always before you think it is.

I did a lot of thinking and planning as I was preparing to start my business (this is good), but very little *doing* (not so good). For months and months, the business existed in my brain and on my MacBook only, not in real life. I did tons of research. I did case studies of other businesses. I had a plan, and I was clear on what I wanted to offer — but then I just sat on it. I didn't feel ready. I didn't know everything yet (p.s. — not possible).

By chance I met a great contact at a coffee shop one day. We both happened to be there reading the same book. He was also a coach and consultant, and so we talked shop about my (still hypothetical) business. He was a close personal friend of a famous business mogul who shall remain nameless. He loved the energy behind the (hypothetical) work I was doing and wondered if I had a business card he could pass along. Nope. Could I write down my website? Nope. Didn't have one.

Fuuuuuuuck.

Talk about a missed opportunity. It was just the kick in the ass I needed to get moving. Over the next two days, I researched web designers and reviewed portfolios. I interviewed two designers and hired one. I had a logo designed. I ordered business cards and marketing materials. I wish I'd done it sooner.

Opportunity knocks, but you won't hear it if you're still tinkering in the basement. At some point, you've got to bring your work out of the darkness and into the light of day. Preferably before an amazing ally shows up and you have to send him away empty-handed.

Finally sharing your work with others is one thing, but getting started is another. If you haven't even started yet, it's time to start. Like, right now. Pronto.

Take the course. Buy the book. Ask for the reference.

Opportunity knocks, but you won't hear it if you're still tinkering in the basement.

Apply for the job. Hire movers. Buy the domain name. Write up a business plan. Take your guitar out of storage. Get your ass to an art supply store. Rent some studio space. Do whatever you have to do to get moving on that thing you want to do but haven't done yet. Start somewhere. Anywhere.

How *much* you sink your teeth into when you start is up to you. You can take a little nibble, or a big hungry bite and let the juice drip down your chin, like eating a peach in peak season right over the kitchen sink. The important thing is that you dive in.

Ideal timing is a figment of our imagination.

But maybe it would be better if you started later, when work isn't so crazy, when your kids aren't so young, after you lose a little weight, or get a little more experience, when the market looks better, when your resume is more impressive, when the timing is better. Right? Wrong.

Waiting for the perfect moment doesn't work because it never shows up. Life is complicated, unpredictable, ever-changing, and always surprising. Ideal timing is a figment of our imagination. Just when you think a window of ideal time is about to open, life will throw you another curveball. Better to start now, even if it means starting very slowly.

I'm a big fan of slow and steady. That tortoise was onto something. Life isn't a race, anyway. I remember I once started a yoga practice and gave up caffeine, refined sugar, and wheat — all in the same day. How do you think that went for me? Yeah. Massive failure. I crashed and burned in less than a week. Slow and steady is where it's at, in life and at work. Just make sure you start.

YOU'RE INVITED
A SEND-OFF

I met my childhood best friend while standing against a red brick wall in a little Catholic schoolyard on the first day of school. I was unbearably shy, and I couldn't work up the courage to go and play with the other kids. A little girl, who I would later learn was named Marcia, ran up to me and said, "Wanna play?" I said yes. She grabbed my hand, and off we rode into the swing set. We were inseparable right up until graduation, and all it took was two little words: *Wanna play?*

Because sometimes it takes an invitation.

Sometimes you desperately want to play, but you can't move your feet. The thought of making a move and joining in is just too much. You can't work up the nerve.

So you stand there, watching from the sidelines. Waiting. Wishing.

If you have felt scared or intimidated or paralyzed or lost in your career, consider this your official invitation. Right here. Right now. I see you. I recognize the longing. I've been where you are. I know what fear and yearning feel like.

Come and play. Find your place among those of us who are happy at work. You're on the team. You're in the club. You already know the secret handshake; you were born with it.

You're invited. Say yes to a future filled with feel-good work.

xo Sarah

Hop over to Careergasm.com
for a free course to help you find
your way to feel-good work.

ACKNOWLEDGMENTS

Martha Beck, you're my Yoda. Thank you for helping me to change my life. Forever grateful, I am. Danielle LaPorte and Linda Sivertsen, thank you for your encouragement, your exquisite brainpower, and for giving me a loving kick in the ass.

Stacy Testa, you took a chance on me and went balls to the wall for this book. All of the artisan chocolate in the world isn't enough to express my thanks. Jen Knoch, you are the unicorn of editors. You make everything sparkly and I can hardly believe you're real. Same goes for the entire crew of magical creatures at ECW Press. I'm so glad I said yes when you asked, *Will you accept this rose?* #truelove

To the people at *Forbes*, *Inc.*, *Entrepreneur*, and *Huffington Post*, early versions of many of these chapters were first published on your pages. Thank you for shining a light on my work. You, too, Leah Eichler. Here's to women helping women. Just because.

To my readers and clients — thank you for trusting me to help you find your way home. One million heart emojis for each of you.

To my tribe of extraordinary women — you know who you are — thank you for holding space for me, for calling me out on my bullshit (only the best kind of friends are willing to do that), and for cheering me on.

Mom, thank you for showing me what feel-good work looks like . . . way before I even knew what that meant. Lots of love to you, Dad, Brian, Ashley, Brad, Dan, and Scott.

Lastly, and most importantly, thank you Phil Rickaby. Your love and support make me feel like I won the lottery. And your good looks and WordPress prowess are just a really awesome bonus.

A former business professor, SARAH VERMUNT is the founder of Careergasm, where she helps people figure out what the heck they want so they can quit jobs they hate and do work they love. She writes about careers for *Forbes*, *Fortune*, *Inc.*, and *Entrepreneur*. She lives in Toronto and online at Careergasm.com.